Go Milk Yourself

You Have Power. Express It!

Francie Webb

FRANCIE WEBB

About the Author

Francie Webb is a mom of two who lives in Harlem, NYC. As founder and CEO of TheMilkinMama, she is dedicated to helping parents have more power, more freedom, and less stress. Francie loved (almost) every minute of the fourteen years she spent teaching middle school, yet she discovered a new calling as a doula and lactation professional after her two transformative births. Francie loves yoga, meditation, reading, writing, traveling, being outdoors, riding her bike, her large extended family, spending time with friends, date nights with her husband, and food.

A native of Virginia who somehow still says "you guys"* instead of "y'all," Francie graduated from Duke University and earned Masters Degrees from Pace University and Bank Street College of Education. She is currently studying to become an International Board Certified Lactation Consultant (IBCLC). Among other aspirations, she hopes to become a midwife one day.

* not gender-neutral, I know! I'm working on it!

FRANCIE WEBB

Table Of Contents

FRANCIE WEBB

Introduction

WoManifesto

Hiiiiiiiiiiii! I'm Francie, TheMilkinMama. That's the name of my business, anyway. I teach hand expression, which basically means getting milk out your boobs with your hands.

My journey—birthing and nurturing this business *and* my two (so far!) children—has been about so much more than hand expression. At the core, it's been about discovering my own power, learning how to access it, and expressing it into the world to nurture myself *and* those around me. Most important, it's been about teaching others to do the same. Throughout this book, I'll refer to this larger journey as the Journey to Enoughness.

If you're here, reading this, it means first and foremost that you're at least somewhat interested in learning about hand expression. And on a deeper level, perhaps you've gotten curious about your own power. Or perhaps you're feeling stressed and helpless and wondering if you have any power at all. All those feelings are understandable! What's more, they're totally normal, no matter who you are or why you're here reading this.

Regardless of how you're feeling about hand expression, seeking out this particular topic takes a certain amount of belief, somewhere inside you, that **there's more where that came from**. Some inkling that you can do something new, something you've perhaps thought you cannot do. Or that you'd like to support someone else in doing what they think they cannot do. In other words, somewhere deep down, you believe that the "impossible" can be made possible. And here you are, 'bout to do it. (Or help someone else do it.) Go you!

For all of this and more, I salute you. Thank you for showing up. Your presence is a gift. Truly. You being here, open to learning big new things, is the most important part, and you've already done it!

And I'm here, writing this book and sharing this knowledge, to support you in this important work.

Now let's get to the rest of it.

What on earth is TheMilkinMama? And why do we exist?

I created TheMilkinMama to empower humans everywhere by teaching hand expression. If you've never heard of hand expression before today, join the club. I sure didn't know that it existed until I was a hot mess of a new mom. Pre-hand expression, I was having frequent toddler-style meltdowns, pumping breast milk alone in an unlocked supply closet at work. (Not totally alone, to be honest. I was with a fridge and a microwave, meaning my colleagues could walk in at any time to, you know, heat up their lunches.) The beginning of my back-to-work-after-baby life was rife with tears. Tears that flowed much more easily than my milk did from my boobs into my pump.

And then I learned to hand express, and it changed everything.

How? That's what this *whole book* is about.

In short, the practice of hand expression supported my move from "I'm a hot mess" to "I've got this," and *mastering* the art of hand expression taught me to believe in myself in a way that I never really had before. In a way I didn't even know I could. I'll tell you much more about all of that later. For now, let's continue with what we do.

On the most basic level, we,[1] through TheMilkinMama, empower humans everywhere by ensuring that all lactating parents[2] have all the options for getting their milk out. If you're feeling confused about how this helps "humans everywhere," stay tuned. I promise we'll get there.

---

[1] TheMilkinMama consists of a team of teachers trained in the Go Milk Yourself Method of teaching hand expression. So far, all of them have been trained by me personally. Some were already lactation professionals before their training; others were inspired to join as a result of their own hand expression practice, which many learned at one of my original Go Milk Yourself online workshops. All of us are connected to our mission; believe in the power of hand expression; help spread the Go Milk Yourself word by teaching workshops and private sessions; and represent our movement at events that promote breastfeeding and chestfeeding. We call our Go Milk Yourself teachers MilkinMamas. (One of our teachers also serves as our Boobsistant, because obviously we needed a *boob*sistant rather than an *ass*istant.)

[2] We define a lactating parent as anyone who's creating milk in their bodies for the purposes of feeding another human, usually a small one. For more on inclusive language, flip a few pages to the section called Inclusivity is Our Priority.

On an even deeper level, we aim to flip the script about how we feed babies with our bodies and how we perceive and care for ourselves. Instead of continuing to buy into the story of stress and scarcity that we've been sold, we invite you to shift into a life of empowerment and abundance. We aim to give you the tools you need to make this shift, so that you can have and do and be whatever it is your badass heart desires, all while feeding your baby (and living your life!) confidently.

See, there are multiple ways of getting your milk out, but most of us are taught only two options: feeding babies directly from the tap (the chest, breast, or boob), and getting milk out with a pump. That's it.

Part of that is because we live in a profit-driven society, and there's a whole industry built around pumping. This industry is based on an expected (and sometimes necessary) separation from baby, and while it helps many (including those whose babies don't drink from the tap, and those of us who spend many hours away from our babies when we go back to work), the prevalence of pumping as the *only* way of feeding baby other than directly from the boob also has effects that are detrimental to parents. The way it's framed in our society, milk becomes a commodity and the most important part of the feeding interaction—more important even than the feeding parent's health and well-being. This reduces the whole thing, this incredible act of feeding a human we created with our own bodies, to a transaction: get your milk out, whatever the cost, and make sure baby gets it. Or don't, because it's all too much. In which case, switch to using formula instead.[3] And if you *can't* do it (feed your baby with milk from your own body), you're made to feel like *the worst parent.*

In *this* world, where pumping is the only alternative to breastfeeding unless you switch to formula, it's all or nothing. The options are served from a prix fixe menu, no substitutions allowed. No control. No power. Definitely no empower*ment.* This system perpetuates a sense that as parents, *we are failing.* We just. Can't. Keep. Up.

We're over it.

In TheMilkinMama world, **YOU get to decide** what way works best for you. Every time.

How does this empower "humans everywhere"? (Told you we'd get here! Woot!)

WE BELIEVE that when a lactating parent knows how to hand express effectively, they have more power, more freedom, and less stress. What's more, we believe that *this shift* changes lives. It quite literally creates a ripple effect

---

[3] Formula. Such a hot topic in parenting circles. Formula is a food for many babies across the world. Some parents feed their babies formula in addition to breastmilk (called combination feeding), and some use formula instead of breastmilk. Many of the parents our MilkinMamas serve use combination feeding, and we support them/you. **You get to decide** what your baby eats, just as **you get to decide** who's on your support team, and precisely what support you need as you navigate parenthood.

from the lactating parent outward, touching everyone they come into contact with. Because, as a lactating parent, when I **know** that I can get my milk out **whenever** I want from **wherever I am** AND *that there is more where that came from*, I AM empowered.

And when I'm empowered? My body responds. My baby responds. My partner and children are nourished by my energy, rather than being traumatized by the tense, nothing-will-ever-get-better, I'm-in-a-hole-and-can't-get-out energies that I transmit when I'm stuck in scarcity (read: stressed about my milk production). When I go out into the world, empowered, my mindful presence impacts friends, colleagues and strangers alike, because I'm living in my most authentic state: enoughness.[4] I feel grounded enough to speak my truth, and to listen to truths of others. I am **a better me**.

Bottom Line: I am more apt to fulfill my purpose in the world when I live inside the *knowing* that I am enough, because *this knowing empowers me* to support others in knowing their own enoughness, too.

---

[4] Enoughness (n.): The opposite of scarcity. Knowing I'm good. "Good" meaning both "a good person" and "I have all that I need." Enoughness feels like breathing easy, and each breath is a relaxing, sustaining one. Living in enoughness also means that you're not trying to do anything more than you can actually do. You're just being. It's like a client recently texted me: "We're not trying to do anything too heroic today." Now *that* is heroic. Being you is all you need, and it's all anyone else needs too. *Also: stay tuned, because there's a lot more on this topic coming up!*

I'll tell you—I haven't always had this empowered existence in my life. Quite the opposite, in fact. For most of my life, I lived in a near-constant state of anxiety, even if it didn't appear that way to others. But since this whole "Go Milk Yourself" thing has come into my life—or, I should say, since it has *become* my life—I've experienced a massive shift. Through practice, the practice of hand expression specifically, I've shifted out of the limiting beliefs, "I must be perfect" and "I'll never be enough," into the more expansive,

"I commit to being present. I commit to practicing. **I am enough**."

I am *always* enough.

How does that feel?

I feel this way, right now, as I write to you.

Enough.

I also feel this way all day, *every single day* of my life, without fail.

PSYCH![5]

That was a lie. I do *not* feel empowered every day without fail.

---

[5] I *really* wanted to spell this "SIKE." Sadly, Urban Dictionary told me not to. But that's how I spelled it back in the '90s, when I was trying to be extra cool.

FRANCIE WEBB

Actually, I'm still quite good at being anxious, worried, even *doomsday* in my thinking, thank you very much. I've had a LOT of practice feeling those things, and to say they don't still come into my daily life from time to time would be an out-and-out lie. Even though I'm writing this book to teach you about hand expression and enoughness, I'm not going to play like I live in this "I am enough" space 100% of the time. That's not my current truth, and I have no interest in keeping up an image of perfection. That wouldn't serve me, and it wouldn't serve you. In fact, it sounds downright exhausting!

Though I've been practicing living this truth—"I am enough"—in my own body for nearly five years now, it's still not uncommon for me to get worked up about something small. Not unusual for me to curse or to call myself Frances out loud, which only one aunt, a few uncles, my best guy friend from high school, and a couple of my exes have *ever* been permitted to do. And from time to time, I still inadvertently take out all of my scarcity issues on my husband. (Sorry, Baby).

All that said...

I do live in enoughness a lot more than I used to. And. When I do slip into feeling not-enough, I recognize quickly that my thoughts are doing "their little show-off dance,"[6] and I can shift those thoughts (read: my whole self and my whole life!) right away. When it comes to helping myself—tapping into my power and using it to shift the way I'm thinking and

---

[6] Mad props to Elizabeth Gilbert for that phrase—I use it all the time. This gem comes from *Eat Pray Love*.

feeling—I've become my own expert. And since I've started teaching Go Milk Yourself to others, I've seen this shift happening in their lives, too. And in the lives of the people in their lives. And so on.

In fact, my friends,

I believe so much in the power of this practice to change lives, that I've dedicated my life to talking about, teaching, and supporting hand expression. And with TheMilkinMama, I've gathered the team I need to help me do just that.

So now that you're abreast of who we are and what we do,

I'd like to share Our Credo.

FRANCIE WEBB

Our Credo

You
are
enough.

That is all.

(That is everything.)

Our Tenets

1. You are enough.[7]
2. You are never alone.[8]
3. There's more where that came from.[9]
4. You get to decide.
5. You are the most important person.
6. You can do the impossible thing.
7. Be your own expert and gather your team.
8. With practice, you have power, and it's all in your hands.

---

[7] Worth saying again. And over and over!

[8] I've considered whether to frame this in the positive, like "you are always supported." I'm a teacher; I get that "We raise our hands to speak" has a totally different feel than "No calling out." I mulled it over and realized that I wanted to include the word *not*, and then expanded that to *never*, because feeling alone is a universal experience. It's also when we are at our most alone that we can feel most transformed by the knowledge that we are, in fact, not alone. So, *never* it is. Not ever, my friends.

[9] We're talking about milk, love, laughter, time, space, wealth, positive energy...

FRANCIE WEBB

What if . . .
1. You didn't need a pump to get your milk out?
2. Going back to work wasn't so stressful?
3. Keeping up with your baby's bottle intake wasn't so anxiety-provoking?
4. Building a freezer stash required much less effort?
5. You could be away from baby without so much baggage?[10]
6. The only thing you had to wash was baby's bottles?

What if . . .
1. You could learn to easily identify and ask for what you need?
2. You had a whole team of people waiting to help YOU meet your needs?
3. You knew exactly whom to ask for what you need?
4. You could care for yourself as well as you care for others without guilt?
5. You felt powerful, capable, and connected to your larger purpose, every day of your life?

Do any (or all!) of the above feel like freedom? If so, then this is the book for you.

Inclusivity is our Priority

We at TheMilkinMama aim to be inclusive of all parents who feed their children, and of everyone who supports parents to that end. It takes a village to do this great work of nourishing and nurturing children, and we intend to honor each and every one of you.

Why is this important to us?

---

[10] Yes, we're talking about *all* the kinds of baggage here, not just pump parts.

Because not everyone who births and feeds babies identifies as a woman; some identify as men, some as femmes, others as non-binary. There are far more identities than I will mention here, and so many more I'm learning as I grow. I will, and do, make mistakes, even though my intention is to be inclusive of everyone. If any words I use trigger you, I'd love for you to come back and refer to our credo and our tenets, in hopes that you'll be reminded of who we are and what we're working to do.

We define a lactating parent as anyone who's creating milk in their bodies for the purposes of feeding another human, usually a small one. For cisgender women, this is typically called breastfeeding. For transgendered men who were born biologically female, the term chestfeeding is used. I choose *lactating* because it is the most inclusive term I currently know for this biological function. I choose *parent* because parents identify as different genders—it's not just women who feed their babies with their bodies. I use the pronoun *they* in this book, unless referring to someone who I know identifies as a woman, because it's the most inclusive pronoun I know. You will see me use *breastfeeding*, *breast*, and *boob* in other parts of this book. I recognize that my use of them is not inclusive of all lactating parents. That said, I chose them in some places because it was simpler to use one term, and they are more commonly used than *chestfeeding* or *chest*. Over time, I have no doubt that more terminology will emerge in the lactation world that will take our desire to be truly inclusive, all of the time, and make it the norm.

This language might make you feel curious, uncomfortable, or some combination of the two. If it does, I encourage you to open up to the many resources about inclusivity online, and really listen to the stories of others whose gender identities differ from yours. We can learn so much from others' experiences.

FRANCIE WEBB

As with most things we do, the language we use at TheMilkinMama (and the language in this book) has evolved over time, and that evolution is reflective of our ongoing learning process. For instance, in earlier versions of the book, I used the word *mama* to describe a lactating parent. Now I know that *mama* doesn't work for everyone. When I hear *mama*, I picture a loving female, cuddling with her child or children, all of whom are wildly, yet quietly, happy to be with her. She's *clearly* doing a great job. (I'm rolling my eyes here, because of the association between "good parenting" and "quiet children!") I know that for many others, *mama* doesn't conjure that same image, those same warm and fuzzy feelings. Quite the opposite, in fact. Thus, I have shifted my language to reflect a wider, more inclusive truth. I'm not about to use *mama* universally, when I know its impact is different on everyone.

Throughout this book, you'll see me use *humans, parents,* and *people* to describe you (all of you reading), the people you support, and others who birth, breathe, lactate, and live in the world. For ease of communication, most often, I've chosen to address the person who's engaged directly in feeding with their body. If you are a support person (doula, midwife, doctor, lactation consultant, partner, family member, friend, or insert-any-other-possible-support-role-here) please know that I've been thinking of you too, as I've written. I'm hopeful that my language—and the knowledge I've offered here—serves you powerfully in supporting those who are lucky enough to have you. Even though I may not always address you directly, you're in my heart.

In the rare instances when I use *mama*, I am describing myself. I use the word consciously, as a term that resonates with me in the places where I've used it.

Finally, I do recognize that I have a whole business with the word *Mama* in the name.[11] Believe me, I know. And it's complex, especially given how strongly I now feel about using inclusive language. (I wonder if we'll change our name to TheMilkinHumans at some point. I guess I'd better go snag that domain before somebody else does!) For now, we continue TheMilkinMama's work, expanding and including even more amazing humans who need us, over time.

I fear that I've over-explained, perhaps gone on too long, in this opening section. And yet, it's important to me to tell it like it is, in all the ways that it is, as clearly as possible, so that we can understand one another. It's important to me that you feel included, because I wrote this book for you. Each and every one of you.

I've done my personal best to be inclusive of anyone and everyone who might possibly lean into this less-than-mainstream topic, and I'm happy to hear from you about how my words resonate with you, or don't.

Also, I'm trusting that what I've done here is enough

because, you know,

enoughness.

Again, thank you for being here with me. We're in this together. (**You are never alone!**) <fist bump emoji>

---

[11] My original business name was The Milkin' Mama, as in, the mama who is always milkin'. Over time, I shifted to TheMilkinMama because, as I began saying, The Milk in Mama is her *POWER*. Not gender-inclusive. But resonated for me at the time, and stuck. We will see what shifts in the future!

FRANCIE WEBB

In all I do, both in my personal life and under the umbrella of TheMilkinMama, my goal is to honor *all* of the ways in which people become parents and *all* of the ways people become *supporters of* parents, regardless of race, class, gender, sexual orientation, religion, ethnicity, nationality, age, illness, disability, or all other forms of identity. My deepest intention is to respect and hear and see you; to communicate with you in a way that works for you and reaches you fully, wherever you are right now.

My intention is to offer my support.

To all of you.

Welcome. I'm *so* glad you're here. I'm deeply honored to share something I love so deeply—with you.

Phew! Let's get to it, now. Shall we?

How to Use This Book

I was going to write a long section about the fact that you can use this book however you want. It was going to be empowering, reaffirming the truth that **you get to decide** by choosing your own adventure and using the tools I give you, however you feel serves you best.

That said, I'm ready to birth this book baby, and I feel like in terms of empowering, I've done enough in the rest of the text.

So here's the gist:

You can read this book start to finish.

You can read parts of this book.

You can get just what you need and go.

You can read one part, be reminded of something else you need, and go get that, before moving on with your life.

You can come back later for whatever you don't yet need.

Throughout the book, I've included a number of footnotes and notes within the text to help direct or redirect you to places where you may find more information you're seeking. Be present to this information as you read, and I'm confident you'll get exactly what you need, exactly when you need it.

FRANCIE WEBB

Chapter 1:
A Badass Book About Breastfeeding

I avoided writing this book for a while.

Like many of you, I've had lots of practice avoiding things that challenge me, and I'm quite good at it! In my house, my favorite things to avoid are dishes and laundry, which drives my husband Leo crazy. He stays on top of both of those. (Thankfully.) Cleaning off the counter before he goes to bed though? Not so much.

Sometimes, Leo leaves an open can of seltzer on the counter overnight.

(See me avoiding? We were at writing, and now we're at seltzer! So fun!)

If the seltzer can ever has anything left in it, it wasn't me. (I love the stuff and drink it like it's, um, water. With bubbles!) But when Leo makes a cocktail (or mocktail) for one of us, or offers some to our daughter in a sippy cup as a bedtime treat, he might pour out a little, then leave the can on the counter and go to bed.

I find these cans when I come into the kitchen the next morning, bleary-eyed and searching for an applesauce pouch to keep our toddler busy for at least one more press of the snooze button. Every single time, I hand over the applesauce to the toddler, pick up the abandoned counter can, and take a sip.

I *know* what's going to happen.

FRANCIE WEBB

It'll be flat,

and I'll be sad.

Still, I give it a whirl. I'm always hoping some miracle will have occurred and *this one can* will have stayed bubbly. Long enough for me to enjoy it. Long enough to ensure that not a drop goes to waste.

Always, it's gone.

What once was, now isn't. And never will be again.

It's been the same with my motivation to write this book. I've been getting all pumped, ready to spill, creating time and space to enjoy letting this stuff bubble up and out and onto the page, only to have my motivation fizzle and die each time I sat down to write. Worse, as I moved through this resistance, every thwarted attempt at a meaningful writing session left me feeling defeated. As though fear had won. I'd let it win.

Now that I'm here, *really* writing, I can see the truth: I wasn't yet ready, because I wasn't yet ready. I had so much more to learn.

You see, at the beginning of all this (back in 2014 when I published *Hand Expression: An Honest Guide to Making the Most of Your Breast Milk*) and in all the time I've been updating it since, I thought I was Right.

Ya know, like, the opposite of Wrong?

What's more, I thought I was here to teach you The Truth. As in, there is only one Right way: to hand express, to parent, to think, to learn, to be. You may relate to this sort of thinking,

2

in which there is a Right and a Wrong way to do things—as if there are only two choices, and we can't see outside of them. But, my friends, what I've finally learned is this: it is simply *not* the case that any one of us is **Right** and everyone else is **Wrong** or that **I Know** and **You Do Not Know**.

Obviously, I have strong beliefs about the stuff in this book, because everything I've shared in here is true for me. What's more, I'm sharing it all with you because I believe that the simple-yet-powerful act of hand expression can change your life. And the lives of everyone you know. And yet, I now also know that what's true for me isn't always true for everybody else. What works for me may not work for everyone. The deepest truth, and what I really needed to learn before beginning my writing in earnest, is that life works best when each of us gets to have power, choice, and freedom.

While I may be the expert on hand expression *and* my own Journey to Enoughness, **you** *always* **get to decide** what works for you. And when I trust you to decide what works for you, I get to show up as the expert I am, share everything that I know, and release the outcome, knowing that I've done enough—for you, for me, for all.

And so, knowing that, and armed with many cans of seltzer (some fizzy, others flat), the support of an incredible team of Go Milk Yourself Teachers (sometimes spelled *Teatchers*, because teats), a badass editor (who promised herself to me far before I was ready), and a commitment to meditate (even for just *one* minute) before each writing session, I got to writing.

After I had finally gotten a good enough chunk of the manuscript done to begin thinking about the logistics of publishing, I called the publishing company. Though I knew I wasn't ready to publish yet, I was feeling the need to tell *someone* I was really doing it. I knew that speaking with

3

another human about the book would help me hold myself accountable; if I called a publishing company, it'd be real. I'd feel as though I'd begun gathering the team that would support me in making this book a reality. So I called.

It wasn't long before the customer service representative asked me what I was writing. I immediately felt nervous. There are two reasons I get nervous when talking hand expression with strangers. First, breastfeeding doesn't go smoothly for everyone, and for many, it's downright traumatic. When I talk about hand expression, I never know if something I say is going to trigger a painful memory for the listener, or if they're going to be completely turned off by me from the get-go, seeing me as a "lactivist"[12] who operates from a place of judgment and shame. These are fears I'm continuing to move through, and thus far, what I've come to understand is that the best I can do is speak my truth and be prepared to listen to another's truth, trusting that if they are triggered by me (which might then trigger *me*), I can find a way to honor both of our truths. Second, despite my growing confidence in my work (also known as, "despite what I share on social media"), a small part of me still worries about what people will think when I say that I teach women to squeeze milk out of their boobs with their hands. Because, you know, they're *boobs*. And that's, like, *gross*.[13]

---

[12] Lactivist (n.): A person who consider themselves an advocate for breast/chestfeeding. In some cases, this term has the connotation of judgment; a lactivist may appear pro-breastfeeding to the point of making those who don't exclusively breastfeed feel bad.

[13] It's actually not gross. Boobs with milk in them are just doing their thing, ya know? What they were made to do. The perception of them as For Sex Only, or On Women's Bodies Yet Made for Men, like so many other things that cause conflict among us, has been constructed over many years by

So I'm on the phone, feeling all this creeping anxiety at talking to this publishing guy, and I'm picturing the man on the other end of the line: a 19-year-old kid who has *maaaybe* seen an aunt nursing a cousin, or heard the women in his family talk about breastfeeding—sharing stories at a baby shower, lamenting how hard it was or how it didn't work out the way they'd hoped, or—and this seemed the most likely scenario in my mind—he knew not one single thing about breastfeeding.

I figured this guy was going to think I was a total weirdo (which I am kind of used to, to be honest), but then I realized, I couldn't *wait* to share my book with him. And with the world. Regardless of what anybody chooses to think or feel about what I have to say.

Deep breath.

I shifted out of fear and into vulnerabravery.[14]

---

culture and corporations and ads for beer and bras and beaches. But yeah, some people think of a liquid coming out of any part of one's body as gross. And a liquid that someone else then consumes? Even grosser. All that said, I'm here to tell you: It's not gross. It's *normal.* #normalizebreastfeeding

[14] Vulnerabravery (n.): the act of being significantly vulnerable and so so brave...at precisely the same time. You're vulnerabrave when you're doing something you thought you'd never do, and when you feel the certainty that you were meant to do exactly this, exactly now. When you put yourself out there and you're scared out of your mind and you also feel your own walls falling down in a way that's thrilling and terrifying and a huge relief and "OH MY GOD IS THIS REALLY HAPPENING?!"—*that's* vulnerabravery. (This is a term I thought I invented that became the basis of my

FRANCIE WEBB

"I'm writing a Badass Book About Breastfeeding."

"I don't think I've ever heard those two words—*badass* and *breastfeeding*—in the same sentence," he responded.

A beat of silence,

and I thought:

Ain't that the truth?!

I asked if he'd ever been around breastfeeding, and he shared that he and his wife have two young children, one of them an infant.

Isn't it funny how just one new insight about someone can change your entire perception of them? The young, inexperienced, and downright clueless-looking kid in my head vanished, and in his place, I saw this grown man, a young father, standing in a dark room. There's just a bit of light seeping in from a nearby hallway, as he takes the baby from his wife for a diaper change. The air is thick with mutual exhaustion. He hands the newly-diapered baby back to her, and then he's running out the door to attend to a crying toddler in another room; she's putting baby back to breast, wondering when she'll steal her next hour of sleep and whether it will even be long enough to count as rest. There's palpable tension in the air of that dark bedroom: a feeling of being swaddled in chaos, of interrupted normalcy.

New parents who know nothing. Old souls who know everything.

---

very first blog post. Later I found that the beautiful writer Toko-Pa coined it shortly before I did.)

I am transported back. Back to a time that seems both ages ago and also like yesterday: the early days of my second daughter's life. The argument at our front door when I thought Leo was taking far too long to get our big girl off to swim lessons. Picture: me, wanting a quiet moment alone before the baby woke up, and he, tired right down to his bones, dragging his feet with our older daughter in tow. The feeling of all of us being totally trapped.

Us, yelling in front of our firstborn. So unlike us, and yet, the default way of being so many humans slip into when we're living in scarcity—in "too much" and "not enough." Our sweet daughter's voice, reminding us: "Daddy, you have to be nice to Mommy." Me having the mother of all meltdowns, in the bathroom after they finally left—alone, so very alone— tears on the toilet, my body still sore from birth, an exhaustion so deep there were no coherent thoughts...only raw, raw feelings. And so many tears. Recalling during my meltdown the phrase, "With the milk come the tears." Wishing it wasn't true.

I remembered it all.

I felt it in my body.

Too much. Not enough.

(And then I remembered I was on the phone.)

I drifted back from my reverie.

I didn't know this man on the other end of the line, but in imagining his experience, I relived my own. I tapped all the way back in to my own feelings of fear and inadequacy. Those feelings I felt so often when I too was parenting a newborn and a toddler. I knew that even as "strangers," this guy and I understood each other perfectly, because we both **know** that breastfeeding is hard. That being a parent is hard. That having a newborn is hard.

That *life* is hard.

I know that this man—not a child but rather the father of two—is the same as me.

That despite our different experiences, he sometimes *feels* like the inexperienced young teenager I originally imagined him to be, just as I have felt inexperienced and ill-equipped so many times on this path of parenthood. I know that this man, just like any person who has been caught in the wilderness of new life, has felt raw and scared and humbled and full of awe. I know that he has witnessed the ups and downs of what it means to feed a baby with one's body. I know that he's experienced deeply the feelings of helplessness, frustration, and anxiety that so many parents go through as they learn to do this big new thing...sustaining a life (or lives!) with their own bodies.

This man responded with eager curiosity when I shared my work with him. Because he's been there. He *gets it*.

We connected.

Later that evening, my new favorite customer service rep followed TheMilkinMama on Instagram. My heart leapt. I knew we'd connected, but a social media follow was far more than I'd hoped for. I felt reassured. I thought, "*This*—writing this book, sharing myself with the world—is *exactly* what I'm meant to be doing right now."

Chapter 2:
Breastfeeding (Life) is Hard

My experience of hand expression (practicing, teaching, and writing about it) has been rife with life lessons, many of which you'll find in this book. I've come to understand these lessons as universal, applying not only to those who are parents, but to anyone who may read this, regardless of the capacity in which you're here. That said, from here on out, I'm going to speak to parents more directly, because that feels easiest to me. Please know that even in moments when you may feel like I'm not speaking directly to you, I believe that everything I say here is applicable *universally*.

Universal lesson number one: We all experience feeling not-enough, and in those experiences, we are all connected. In fact, this is the very thing that created such an immediate and powerful connection with my customer service rep: we connected because we both know that when there's a brand new baby, there are so many moments when it feels as though *no one is winning*. (Except maybe the baby, who's being fed and changed and cleaned and cared for.)

In moments like that, and any moment of not-enough, really, it can feel as if the "hard" will always outweigh the "awesome." And of course, it does, sometimes. When you're a new parent, everything from hormones to relationship dynamics to time and space has shifted, suddenly and quite significantly, and on top of that, *everyone* is exhausted. No one knows what they need or how to communicate it, and every member of the family who's old enough to do so, feels inadequate.

But there are also magical moments, when we're lucky. When we're present enough to experience them fully.

FRANCIE WEBB

For Leo and me, in the weeks and months following our front-door showdown:

The deep quiet, when baby was sleeping and we sat together, admiring her beautiful little being. Or when we *actually*, as The Experts always recommend, slept when the baby slept. The rare evenings we got to watch a movie together in unexpected luxury, one child sleeping in her room and the other passed out on one of our chests. The moments when we reveled in the beautiful mess—the room in chaos but the air rife with new love—sitting in the sauce of "Look! Look what we made!"

Yes, everyone's parenting experience is unique. And. I'm willing to bet that most have experienced some combination of immense pleasure and powerful discomfort. Even more so, I'm certain that all of us (non-parents included) have experienced that deep sense of inadequacy and failure that lives inside the body in those moments when the hard is outweighing the awesome:

I. AM NOT. ENOUGH.

No matter how hard I try, I just am not. And I never will be.

WE. ARE NOT. ENOUGH.

No matter how hard we try, we just are not. And we never will be.

I believe this experience is universal.

And I *know* that not-enough is a feeling that's hard to shake.

It's a feeling that can come roaring back to life anytime things get challenging. Anytime we feel like we're failing. Anytime we begin remembering all the *other* times we felt like we were failing. (Universal experience of the not-enough downward spiral, anyone?)

I also believe that when you're entrusted with the care of a tiny human, these experiences can occur even more frequently than in normal, non-parenting human life. And breastfeeding, which can be stressful even under the best of circumstances, can contribute mightily to the problem—to these feelings of inadequacy—especially for those who are actually doing the work of feeding a baby with their body.

Because here's the truth: breastfeeding can be really easy, but it can also be really freaking hard. Whether it's just a few touch-and-go moments or pretty much the whole experience that's challenging, it's truly a dance that requires you to relax and surrender. I want to be clear that relaxing and surrendering isn't always an easy thing to do, and yet, when we do both, things go better for us.

It's kind of like...life.

When I'm all, "Why is this happening to me?" and I feel like I'm fighting against my circumstances, things suck extra. When instead I surrender to exactly what's happening and focus on being present in the experience, the fight in me goes away, and it creates space for better things: a quieter mind, unexpected learning, and meaningful change, just to name a few. It creates an opportunity for me to dance through the challenges I'm facing, whatever they may be.

For some people, the dance of breastfeeding comes easily, but in my conversations with the hundreds of lactating parents I've supported all around the world, I've heard, "Wow, I had no idea how hard that was going to be," far more often than I've heard, "That was a breeze!" Because, just like any dance, breastfeeding is an experience where two humans (or more!)[15] are finding a rhythm together. Regardless of the circumstances, this takes time, practice, and a willingness to adapt. Even if you've done the dance before and remember the steps, with a new partner, there are always adjustments to be made if you're going to dance together with ease. Heck, even with the same partner, we gotta make adjustments!

Regardless of how many times you've danced the dance (and really, no matter which dance in life we're talking about), things are always shifting. Someone steps on someone else's toes. One of you is moving faster than the other. The music stops or the song changes, just when you've hit your groove. One of you stumbles, even falls. The dance challenges you, over and over again, to *just be in it*. Some days, the effort exhausts you and you go to bed feeling like shit, positively dreading the next dance. But every now and then, when the stars align, you experience flight. Like that moment when Patrick Swayze finally catches Baby in the perfect lift, and the crowd goes wild.

Your heart soars as you just...

feed your baby.

And you know:

You were made for this moment.

Hopefully, moments like this become your norm, but as with most things, learning to ace it every time takes a commitment to practice. The good news is that **with practice, you have power, and it's all in your hands.**

---

[15] Shout out to tandem-feeding parents and those with multiples!

For some, finding a groove never happens. They stop breastfeeding without ever having the chance to experience that feeling of flight. They might stop because it's all too much. Because they've tried and it's just not working, for either or both of them. Or because life happens—an illness, an inexplicable nursing strike or dip in production, a major life stressor—something that turns all the plans upside down. Some might move away from the boob: to pumping only, to donor milk, to formula, to some combination of these options. For others, there's a moment when the steps start to become second nature, and feeding baby becomes something that you both can just *do.* Together. Because you've practiced. You've learned the basic steps and now, you are in sync enough to find your way into new ones. Together. And finally, there are parents who persevere, suffering through breastfeeding or pumping for their babies, even though it sucks the *whole* time, because the support they need to shift into dance mode is simply not there. They persist, but it continues to feel more like a combination of awkward and painful steps than a real *dance.*

No matter where you are in your present breastfeeding/parenthood/life journey, what I want to tell you is this: no matter how awkward and painful it may be feeling right now, **YOU ARE ENOUGH. And you are never alone.** What's more, with practice and support, this process of learning to feed your baby with your body (and moving through all the things that come up as you do that) *can **ignite*** the process of your own transformation. You may have already consciously begun your Journey to Enoughness, and if you haven't, practicing hand expression may be the first step on that path.

If that's what you choose. **You get to decide.**

If for any reason you're reading this and using hand expression to jump-start your Journey to Enoughness doesn't resonate for you, by all means, pick something else to practice! Because **with** *any* **practice, you have power, and it's all in your hands.** The point is that **you get to decide.**

Chapter 3:
Hand Expression Changed *Me*

For me, starting to hand express wasn't the first conscious step on my Journey to Enoughness. I'd been on that journey for quite some time already when I learned to squeeze milk out of my boobs. [16] It's also worth mentioning that breastfeeding *alone* totally changed my life. But hand expression has been *crucial* on my journey. It's been the key to a kind of freedom I never thought possible.

Why?

Because I've been where many of you are right now: terrified of not having enough milk; of being separated from baby; of something happening to one of us; in pain; riddled with anxiety; perpetually sleep-deprived (because, well, babies).

---

[16] Fun fact: my first business email address was squeezeyourboobs@gmail.com. I really wanted "gomilkyourself@gmail.com," but somebody already had it. (WHO HAS THAT EMAIL ADDRESS, AND WHAT ARE THEY DOING WITH IT?!) Anyway, "squeezeyourboobs" worked for a little while, but eventually, I realized...that phrasing perpetuates an idea that no longer feels like a match for me: the idea that hand expressing has to be physically stressful. I mean really, who wants to "squeeze" already-tender boobs? And even if they're not tender, the very word "squeeze" connotes tension in the hands, which is no good. When we teach you to Go Milk Yourself, *we* aim to be as relaxed as possible, and we want that to be true for *you*, too. And so, our current email address is info@themilkinmama.com, just in case you need to reach us.

FRANCIE WEBB

I'm proud to say:

I'm not there anymore, and it's *not* because I'm no longer breastfeeding. In fact, my second daughter is still going strong at age 2, which means I've been breastfeeding almost continuously for over half a decade.

So, other than learning how to squeeze milk out of my boobs, what's changed?

In simplest terms, I don't worry about feeding my baby anymore. I just do it. Because of hand expression, I know *without a doubt* that I can get milk out whenever I want, wherever I want, using only my hands, if that's the best tool that's available. As a result of that knowing, my breastfeeding experience is now one of relative ease. When I'm with my toddler, I nurse her. When I'm not, I either wait it out (since my nursling is old enough for this *and thus* my body can handle it), or I hand express.

This shift isn't just about my boobs and what's coming out of them—this change has affected my whole life. It's been a shift out of worry and doubt, into knowing and faith.

Hand expression has changed my life,

because now I know:

I am enough.

For my family.

For my loved ones.

For the people I serve.

And for the person who's most important:

my own *self.* [17]

If you've read this whole chapter, and you're still not getting how hand expression changed my life, read on. In the next chapter, I'll share all the nitty gritty details. If you're ready to learn hand expression already (yay!), turn to Chapter 5 to find everything you need to know.

---

[17] Read more about **the most important person** in the section of that name in Chapter 6.

FRANCIE WEBB

Chapter 4:
Hand Expression Changed My *Life*

(aka – That Time I Learned to Squeeze Milk Out of My Boobs with My Hands)

My hand expression journey began, as so many journeys do, with a total and udder mama meltdown.

It was my second day back at work after having my first baby, and I had a problem: I wasn't pumping enough. The (very) small freezer stash I'd compiled before heading back to work was already gone. Our caregiver was requesting more milk for the next day, and I didn't have it.

I realized, only two days in, that I wasn't up to the task of doing it all: keeping up with baby's appetite, dealing emotionally with being apart from my newborn, *and* giving the job I'd loved for so many years my all.

In a full-on frenzy, I showed up at a store in Manhattan—which I've since decided has the best name ever, The Upper Breast Side[18]—and broke down. The owner assured me that I would be okay, and so would my baby. Two hours, a box of tissues, and at least three hugs later, I left the store—with a hospital grade pump, two sets of pump parts, and a list of things to try to maximize my milk production.

I spent the next few weeks trying:

---

[18] Because it's on the Upper West Side. And that's just *awesome*.

19

adding another pump session each workday,

pumping as soon as I got to work,

buying a hands-free pumping bra,

taking fenugreek,

drinking more water,

massaging and compressing my breasts while pumping,

drinking *more* water,

thinking about and looking at pictures of my baby while nursing.

All the things.

With each new trick I tried, there was *some* improvement, sure—a little more milk in the bottles attached to my pump—but only at first. Soon after I started to feel hopeful, things leveled off. It was as if my production was plateauing each time as my body adjusted to each new tool.

Yes, I was leaving work with more milk for baby each day, but I still wasn't feeling good. Pumping was taking a ton of time and energy, both mentally and physically. And (isn't there always an *and?*) I was wanting even more milk than usual for my freezer supply, because I was planning a few days away from baby. A trip to Ojai for my annual yoga retreat.

Are you sensing the scarcity here? The not-enoughness? Both at work and at home, anxieties about milk consumed my mind. My days. My nights. My life.

Feeling desperate once again, I called The Upper Breast Side and spoke with the lactation consultant on call.

"I'm still not pumping enough."

She ran me through a list of questions, asking what I had tried.

I was already doing it *all*. I promised.

Just when it seemed we might be at a loss, she suggested I watch a video: "Maximizing Milk Production with Hands-On Pumping."[19] It was linked on the store's website and showed, among other things, women squeezing *extra* milk out of their boobs with their hands after they'd finished pumping.

At the time, I didn't know the term *hand expression* or anything else about it. I'd heard in my breastfeeding support group that massaging before pumping was sometimes helpful, and I'd once gotten a few squirts out in the shower just to see if I could (and been like, "*Whoa* this is weird"), but I had *no* idea that anyone could get any significant amount of milk out using only their own two hands (or even *one* hand!).

It's a well-made video, and I watched with my jaw all the way down to my boobs, aghast. To my anxious, new-mama self, it was overwhelming. The women had boobs the size of my head, and as they pressed upward around their nipples, milk came cascading out, like a waterfall. (Milkfall?) I felt hopeful

---

[19] This is a well-known video produced by Dr. Jane Morton at Stanford University. It's not about hand expression specifically, but about getting more milk while pumping. Later I learned that she also made a video on hand expression, but I didn't know about it at the time.

for a brief moment, but then crestfallen as self-realization came crashing down.

I knew. There was *no way* I could do *that*.

Impossible.

With nothing else to try, though, I decided to give it a shot. I pumped as normal at work (perhaps massaging and compressing a bit more thoughtfully beforehand though, based on what I'd seen the head-sized-boobed women do), but at the end of my pumping session, I turned off my pump, unplugged the tubes, and held my breast over the flange.

And I squeezed.

I don't know if even a single drop came out with that first squeeze, but I kept trying. After a few minutes, I had expressed a few extra drops. *Well, at least that's something*, I thought.

This seemingly tiny moment of mediocre success quickly led to an even greater awareness: *There's more milk in there. I just need to find a way to get it out.*

As soon as I realized there might be more milk where those few drops came from, I felt determined. I was ready to learn this new dance, and I felt hope where there once was none. It was like magic. The impossible was now possible. I started to feel excited. Learning this new dance of hand expression might make my *whole life* easier. I didn't want to get my hopes *all the way* up, but I was excited nonetheless.

Over the next few days, I tried the same tactics repeatedly, and soon, I was getting a measurable amount—first ⅛, then

¼, and soon, ½ oz—just by massaging and squeezing in a post-pump guess-and-check.[20]

My suspicion had been confirmed.

There was, in fact, more in there.

More where that came from.

It felt like bonus milk! And I loved it. I had never imagined I could actually get milk out without the pump OR the baby, and this discovery—that there was power in my very own hands—changed everything.

Until then, I'd been pumping every weeknight around 10 PM, right before I went to bed and during a longer stretch of baby's sleep. I hated pumping in general, but that last pump of the day was downright dreadworthy. By that point, I was (as I now say to my five-year-old), "the tiredest of the mommies." Just so *done*.

Late one night shortly after my discovery, I was enjoying some TV time with Leo. I was feeling exhausted from a long day at work, and the last thing I wanted to do was hook *that machine* up to my nipples. So I decided to try getting milk out with just my hands. I grabbed a bottle to squirt into and started doing my thing while continuing to focus on our show.

In just seven minutes, I had two ounces!

---

[20] In case you've never heard of a guess-and-check process, it's when you try something, see how it goes, and adjust as needed. You feel like you're going in blind, but you give it a go anyway and slide into your own learning.

FRANCIE WEBB

I was shocked

and *thrilled*.

Pumped, my friends.

Pumped![21]

While also pump-*freeeeeeeee*!

A few nights later, my girl slept through the night quite randomly, and my engorged boobs woke me up before she did. I snuck into the bathroom of our tiny one-bedroom apartment and got to work massaging and compressing my boobs. In about 12 minutes,[22] I had four ounces of milk. In the bottle! This was a revelation. Four ounces was enough for a full feeding, *plus* a little extra!

More than enough.

I started feeling like I was really getting somewhere at that point, and in retrospect, I realize that I was beginning to sense my own deep reservoirs of enoughness. I didn't yet fully trust in myself and this new process, but something was shifting. I could feel it.

I continued my usual routine with the pump at work, still thinking of my new trick (hand expression *without* pumping first) as something to use occasionally—perhaps in cases of

---

[21] We LOVE puns at TheMilkinMama. Send us your puns! We're always trying to think of more that are relevant to our work.

[22] I might be getting the number of minutes wrong here. It *might* have been 9. But *damn*—I could do it! And it didn't take anywhere close to the time I'd spend on the pump!

emergency. My anxiety lessened a bit knowing I could choose not to pump every now and then when I really didn't feel like it, *and* that I could get bonus milk out after every pumping session. All that said, for some reason, I still didn't really consider ditching the pump entirely. I'm sure I didn't believe that I could. Before I knew it, I'd been back at work for seven weeks, successfully feeding baby through this combo of methods, and I was feeling pretty good.

I was soon off on my trip to Ojai, with a plan to leave baby (and all that hard-earned bonus milk!) with my in-laws. My pump was packed safely in my suitcase, right next to my yoga mat. And while I was still a little stressed when baby needed a bottle on the car ride to the airport and I had to give up some of that precious bonus milk earlier than expected, I was at least a tit bit more relaxed about the milk now that I knew how to go milk myself. Feeding her a bottle in the car was a slight annoyance, but it didn't trigger a dive headfirst into panic mode.

We arrived safely on the west coast, spent the night with the grandparents, nursed together one last time, and then, I hopped in my friend Emily's Prius. We zoomed off toward our yoga retreat, ready for some zen.

As we pulled onto the freeway, I realized there was a problem:

I'd left my pump parts at home.

THE WORST.

(Not leaving your pump parts at home, specifically.)

FRANCIE WEBB

THE WORST is that feeling you get when you know exactly what you need, and you *also* know that you don't have it and you can't get it, and all is just...lost.

I imagined my pump parts sitting right where I must have left them...on my dining table.

Those *damn* pump parts. So many parts. Too much! (Not enough!)

I began sliding down the rabbit hole of anxiety (a familiar place of some perverse comfort at that time, I'll admit), all my scarcity issues rearing their ugly heads. I didn't know how to deal. I was traveling fast, back to Not Enough.[23] I could feel it happening.

I didn't yet know how to help myself out of that downward spiral, so I did the only thing that made any sense: I spoke my panic aloud to Emily. Emily, who had known me since we were children at summer camp together, and who'd seen me through all sorts of life challenges. Emily, who was looking forward to our zen time together just as much as I was.

"How am I supposed to get milk out *now*?!"

She gave me a funny look.

"Wait, France,[24] don't you know how to get it out with your hands???"

---

[23] I'm capitalizing this, here and throughout, because Not Enough feels like a place we go and visit. Like a town! Or a state! (and it *is*, in fact, a state!) We visit, and sometimes we stay there. And *that* really sucks!

[24] She calls me *France*, and no, you can't.

26

"Yeah," I replied, "but not like *that*."

Despite the fact that I'd been routinely expressing post-pump and had succeeded in those two sans-pump times I described earlier, I still didn't have confidence that I could use *only* my hands the *whole* weekend, and still get the milk out. I felt sure that my boobs would explode and I would...die? I don't know. I just *knew* that I wouldn't make it.

Knowing there was no way to get pump parts where we were going, Emily and I talked through options. We agreed that I would *try* to get the milk out with my hands, with the caveat that if we got desperate, we could drive the hour and a half to my in-laws' house, or ask them to meet us partway, so I could nurse the baby, and we'd decide what to do from there.

I was itchy with anxiety (my go-to symptom), but with a plan and Emily's support, I trusted that we'd make *something* work. That my boobs wouldn't fail me. That I wouldn't fail them, either.

24 hours later, I had 29 ounces of beautiful golden milk, all hand expressed.

Every 3ish hours—if you were on that yoga retreat with me (and it'd be cool if you were!)—you could find me sitting in a chair outside class, or even in the back of class, massaging, squirting, and collecting, raising the bottle to the light to see—Look!—how much I'd made.

I was so damn proud.

In fact, I had Emily take a picture of me counting my milk, and we joked about how it felt like we were counting our millions we'd scored in an *Oceans Eleven*-like scheme!

Old-School Photo: Counting My Milk in Ojai

I thought back to the moment I'd packed *all my bonus milk* and how I'd schlepped it on the trip. I remembered feeling as if I'd never been prouder of anything in my life up to that point as I was of having created all that extra - except, perhaps, of creating my child herself. But this? This was even bigger.

I'd gotten all this magic milk out, and I'd done it *all by myself*.[25]

---

[25] My mom says that my first sentence was, "I can do it myself." I always call this, the propensity to want to do everything myself and to be immensely proud of myself when I do, the biggest blessing and greatest curse of my life. I'm fiercely independent, some might say headstrong; I have also struggled to ask for help and to relax into the support others can provide. And yet, as you'll see as you continue to

I successfully hand expressed for the entirety of my time away from baby, and I was barely even fazed when my in-laws panicked, bringing baby up for lunch one day because they feared they would soon run out of bottles. I didn't need to panic. I had plenty to give them. I'd expressed 29 ounces in the first 24 hours alone!

More than enough.

Over the course of that fateful weekend, I further internalized the truth I'd already begun to sense:

There's always more where that came from,

and

I can get it out *whenever I want!*

I returned home a new woman—a new *me.*

I still wasn't ready to break up with my hospital-grade pump—at that point I was using the Medela Classic, which looks like a mini-factory housed in industrial plastic and metal[26]—but I did decide to try going without it at work, just

---

read, I've gotten better at both of these very important things!

[26] Seriously, go look it up on Google Images right now. I'll wait...I mean *I know.* Right?! Can you believe it's something designed to pull your milk out of your nipples?! It *does* get milk out quite effectively for some. But *sheesh.* I recently asked the members of TheMilkinMama Support Group, an online community for our clients, to take a look at this same image and then answer the question, "If you didn't know what this was, what would you think it was?" Answers included: a device for time travel, a centrifuge, some piece of

to see. I soon found that I didn't need the pump at all, and about a month after our trip, I returned it to The Upper Breast Side.

On a random weekday off soon thereafter, I showed back up at the breastfeeding group, positively pumped to tell my favorite lactation consultant, Andrea, what I'd learned.

"I can get the milk out with my *hands.*"

Looking at my proud, still-astonished face, Andrea smiled.

"Of course you can! It's called hand expression. But I must say: I've never seen *anyone this* excited about it!"

And that's how it all began. I started spreading the word:

Go Milk Yourself.

---

science lab equipment, a coffee machine, an ice cream machine, a food processor that belongs in a factory, part of the original computer, a seismometer, a pump to put air in a tire, and "some kind of jacked up music box."

Chapter 5:
How to Hand Express

If you're ready to learn how to hand express, this is the section for you. If instead, you'd like to continue reading about my Journey to Enoughness, skip to Chapter 6. You can always come back and learn the hand expression basics when you're ready.

Before we truly dive in, let me first say: I did not invent hand expression. You probably knew that already, and yet I'd like to emphasize it here. Humans have been hand expressing for years (possibly forever), because nature endowed us with this gift. Even without hard data to prove it, I'm pretty sure hand expression has been around since breasts and hands were, um, invented. Electric pumps weren't widely available until the 1990s, so unless you were in a hospital that had access to pumps, hands were the go-to method for anyone wanting to get milk into a vessel that wasn't a baby's mouth.

More than once, I've had a woman approach me to tell me she hand expressed years ago, and she usually shares one of two things:

1. "I'm so glad pumps were invented—mothers today don't know how lucky they are!"
2. "I never needed a machine! We're so dependent on machines these days."

It's amazing to me that this idea of hand expression is so normalized for these women. When I began breastfeeding, I didn't even know that there was another way to get milk out, besides the baby or a pump. I'd never heard of getting milk out with your hands as an option! It wasn't until I saw the head-sized-boob-squeezing video that I'd opened up to this new possibility of squeezing milk out of my own boobs, and even then, I had a lot of doubts about it working. Thankfully, I was still curious enough to try it out, despite my reservations. (Alert! Alert! Life lesson in there!)

I am so grateful that I came across this option, which so many women throughout history have relied upon. And from that gratitude, my desire to learn about hand expression—my curiosity and reverence around the process—deepened. I began to teach.

Before long, I developed the Go Milk Yourself Method, a menu of techniques that provide entry points for anyone who wants—or needs—to hand express. Some of these techniques I've discovered along the way; others I read about on the interwebs; others were taught to me by clients, professionals, or complete strangers. (**I am never alone!**)

In this book, I've rolled the basics of what I know right now—everything I think you need to know to be successful at hand expression—into a list of approaches. It's my intention to offer an accessible resource for each of you within these pages. **You get to decide** what works for you. What's more, it's your responsibility to find your own way. Don't take my word as Truth on this stuff. Try it out. Play with the techniques. Discover *your* way to hand express (and to LIVE!).

What you'll find in the rest of this chapter will help you get started, support you in refining your process, and inspire you in trying some new tricks when you get stuck (or when the milk does—ouch!).

It's worth saying that the process of feeding your baby with your body can feel lonely. Sometimes, learning to hand express can feel lonely, too. This might be because not many people you know are doing it, or you may have come to this book because you are already experiencing some breastfeeding challenges. I'd like to take this moment to remind you that **you are never alone**. Whatever you are going through right now, please know that we are here for you, and all it takes is one email to be one step closer to getting support that can change your life.

Hand Expression Basics

Before you get started, you'll want to wash your hands well and to make sure you have a clean vessel: a bottle, bottle with pump parts attached, measuring cup, mug, Breastbowl[27] (my favorite!), measuring cup, mixing bowl, empty water bottle, leftover Cool Whip container from your grandmother's house. Whatever you've got!

Now, it's time to get into position.

Whether we're hand expressing, pumping, or feeding our babies straight from the tap, it's important to be mindful of posture, because the way we hold our bodies is important. (#MoreLifeLessons) Posture has a huge effect on us in any circumstances; it can support us in feeling great, awful, or anywhere in between. Posture can also be a symptom of other experiences we are having within our bodies—we might be tense or in pain, and our posture reflects this. However, the coolest part about the mind-body connection is that it goes both ways: by simply being mindful of our posture, we can encourage relaxation in our bodies. We carry enough tension in our bodies already; we don't need to add any more with crappy posture while expressing our milk.

---

[27] A Breastbowl is a vessel made specifically for the hand expression of breastmilk. You can read more about them in the Resources section.

When you're setting up to hand express, make sure you:
1. Sit comfortably.
2. Keep your shoulders back and down, away from your ears.[28]
3. Keep your joints straight and body as relaxed as possible, from neck to fingertips.[29]
4. Adjust as needed. Always.[30]

Ready? Great.

First, know this: strong hand expression skillz (yup, I said it) are built on only two basic ideas: massage and compression. It may sound like an oversimplification, yet it's totally true. If you rely on these two things, and trust them to carry you, you will be successful.

---

[28] Tip: Many a great yoga teacher has taught me to scrunch my shoulders up tight by my ears, then let them drop back and down. This move may help guide you to a comfortable starting position.

[29] Elbows down, wrist straight, fingers never making a claw shape...always relaxed. Arms, hands, wrists, and fingers *all* free of tension. (Or as free of tension as it's possible for you to get. Remember, all of this is a process, so you may learn to relax more deeply as you go.) Advanced practice: extend that relaxed energy all the way down to your toes and use hand expression as time for a whole-body meditation. Extra advanced practice: Use a guided relaxation video (on YouTube) or app (like Insight Timer) for a supported experience.

[30] When you notice tension as you Go Milk Yourself—and you will—take a moment to re-relax. (What if we did this all the time in our lives?! The life lessons continue!) Find the balance between doing what you need to get your milk out and also totally chilling out. It'll work, I promise. (If it doesn't, keep trying! It's a practice.)

The very first time I taught another parent to hand express, I forgot to teach this very important concept: massage and compression work in concert.

I came home from my first private session with this parent feeling accomplished and inspired. She had hand expressed successfully and was feeling curious enough that I knew she'd continue practicing and honing her technique. She texted me later that night to tell me she loved not needing to use the pump, but she didn't love how long it was taking to hand express.

"I massaged for 20 minutes, then compressed for 25. Will it always take this long?"

In our session, we'd gone through massage moves—I modeled and she practiced—and then compression moves—again, I modeled and she practiced. But we didn't move through a whole cycle of hand expression together, so she didn't have the chance to see that **massage and compression work in concert.** I inadvertently presented these as two very separate actions...one that starts and finishes, followed by another that starts and finishes, rather than demonstrating how the techniques work in tandem to support in the expression of milk (and badassery).

Let me tell you right up front here, instead of having only one massage period followed by a compression period (as you might do if you're massaging before pumping, which I totally recommend), you are meant to alternate massaging and compressing throughout the time that you are hand expressing.

Now that we've got that very important context covered, let's get down to boobness.

Massaging: Everything You Need to Know

Massage helps you do three things:

1. Bring the milk forward and down (You can tell it where to go!).
2. Stimulate letdown[31] (if and as needed).
3. Reach all ducts.

I'm a big advocate for massaging *both before and during* hand expression. In TheMilkinMama workshops,[32] we teach that effective hand expression is at least 51% massage and up to 49% compression.[33] The belief is that when you massage,

---

[31] The release of milk within the breasts—the moment when the milk says, "I'M COMING OUT! (I want the world to know…)" Some parents experience this as a tingly sensation or even a painful one. Some can see it when pumping or hand expressing—it's when the floodgates appear to open. Others don't feel or see it at all.

[32] At TheMilkinMama, we teach virtual and in-person workshops to lactating parents and those who support them. At the time of this writing, we offer 1-2 workshops a month, all taught by trained MilkinMamas. In about one hour, we teach the basic and specialized techniques of the Go Milk Yourself Method, and give you time and space to practice and ask questions. We also offer private sessions and custom workshops for interested groups, either from the comfort from your own home or in another location that feels good. Soon, we will be offering videos of specific techniques to make Go Milk Yourself even handier for all.

[33] This teaching philosophy, 51% and 49%, comes from my 14 years of teaching middle school, during which I leaned into the belief that the best teachers teach 51% Character, 49% Academics. These numbers, taught to me by educators I still admire greatly, are an expression of the deeper truth that who you are is more important than how you perform.

whether before or during hand expression, now that you've let the milk know where you want it to go, it may be more "ready" to come out.

Personally, I've found this to be true. Massaging helps me tell my milk where to go—forward and down—and then, my milk comes out more easily. It's like I'm saying: "Hey milk! I love you. Come this way. Let's do this together." Is this more psychological than physiological? I don't really know, and to be honest, I don't really care.[34] I just know that I get more streams, steadier streams, and overall higher output when I massage, and I believe massage will benefit you too.

Do you *need* to massage? Depends. If milk is dropping out of you like it's hot, you might be able to skip straight to compression. However, if that's not the case, massage first. And remember, you can always come back to massage if and when the streams and sprays turn to drips and drops, or if the flow stops altogether.

That working to improve yourself and being good to others is a higher priority than whatever you produce.

[34] Massaging before compression is like stimulation mode on a pump. You're stimulating the milk ejection reflex (MER). I won't go into the science too much here, but **you get to decide** what more you want to know about this, so feel free to dig in and learn more as you see fit!

Select Methods for Massage[35]

The methods listed below are all meant to get you started as you develop your own unique practice. As you use them, keep in mind that it's important to do what feels good to you and that there is no Right way to do this. Feel empowered to play around. If you don't know where to start with that, try any of the listed massaging motions with two hands instead of one, particularly if your breasts are too large to get one hand around.

Regardless of which massage method you choose, notice any areas your hands come across that feel fuller or have more friction or even lumps; this sensory information supports you. Pay extra attention to these areas, and try out different pressure as you learn what works best for you. Always, feel free to spend extra time on any area that's wanting it.

---

[35] This section begins the part where I'll explain the How of hand expression techniques. I've included some photos as well. Since these photos are most likely not you, it won't look exactly the same when *you* Go Milk Yourself. Each of us learns differently, so if you find that you need more than what's in this book to learn hand expression, I invite you to head to our website where you'll find videos and many more resources to support you. **You are never alone!**

1. The C-Shape[36]

Make a C-shape with your thumb as the top of the C, and your other four fingers as the bottom of the C. This can also be considered a U-shape if you rotate it, and is sometimes known as the "smiley." Use whatever shape (and shape name) feels best for you and is most comfortable for your wrists.

Start with your C at the base of your breast(s),[37] close to your armpit and breastbone, with your curved palm (the curve of the C) either touching or close to your breast. If your breast were a clock, you can imagine that you'd start with your thumb close to midnight and fingers near six. Move your C forward and down towards your nipple. The inside of your fingers will be gliding along your skin. Once you've moved all the way down to your nipple, move your hand to the starting position and begin again. Keep doing this, moving your C around to reach different areas of the breast and rotating to maximize your comfort. To get to the inside of your breast,

---

[36] Although I started calling this "the C-shape" in my own head, this term is not unique to the Go Milk Yourself Method. The suggestion to form a C is also used in the Marmet Technique, which is named after a wonderful lactation consultant, Chele Marmet, and is perhaps the best-known technique for hand expression. She also recommends rolling your thumb, which you will see later in this chapter. You can find out more about the Marmet Technique with a quick internet search, and see how it goes for you.

[37] From this point on you will hear me use breast and breasts interchangeably; **you get to decide** what moves to try with one breast or both at the same time. All massage and compression moves are possible with one or two hands, as long as you have a place to hold or rest the vessel you are expressing into.

you can use the other hand, or move your thumb to the inner side, and use a pulling motion with your C.

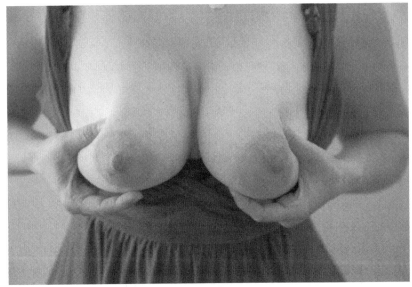

The C-Shape

2. The Heel of Your Hand[38]

Find the heel of your hand—that broad space where the bottom of your hand meets your wrist. Imagine that your breasts are divided into four quadrants, perhaps north, south, east, and west, if that analogy works for you. Keeping your wrist as relaxed as possible, place the heel of your hand at the top of your breast close to the breastbone. (If you're going with the four directions analogy, this is the "north" position.) Move the heel along the breast to the nipple, with

------

[38] This technique was taught to me by Andrea Syms-Brown of Baby in the Family, LLC, who is an IBCLC in NYC (wow! That's a lot of Cs!). She also happens to be my favorite lactation consultant and my mentor. You can read more about her in the Resources section.

gentle pressure, almost like a pushing motion. Use a similar motion along the side of your breast close to your armpit. On the southern quadrant, underneath your breast, your fingers may point upward toward your face or downward toward your waist, depending on the size and shape of your breasts, and the motion may feel more like pulling than pushing. On the inside quadrant, try using the opposite hand, or turning your hands so your fingers point upward toward your face (almost like a one-handed prayer position), allowing you to use a pulling motion to move down toward the nipple. Continue moving around the four quadrants in whatever order feels natural for you.

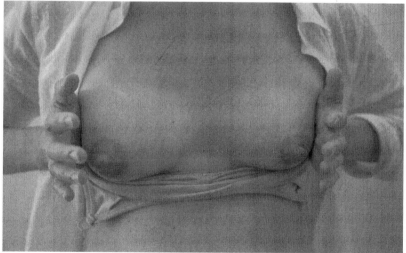

The Heel of Your Hand

3. The Spatula[39]

Imagine that your hand is a spatula. Take all of your fingers and your thumb and pull them close together so that your hand is flat and strong. Envision your breast as a bowl of brownie batter, and make it a goal to get all of the batter out of the bowl. Using the edge of your handmade spatula (I prefer the outer edge, the pinky side, but sometimes the inner edge works well too), move from the breastbone down to the nipple, moving around to ensure you don't miss a single spot, just as you wouldn't want to miss a single lick of your favorite brownie batter.

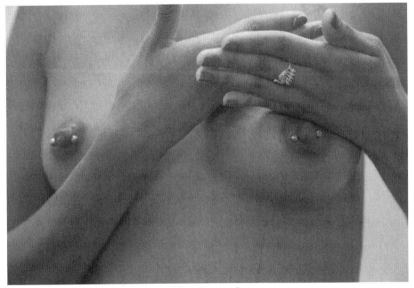

The Spatula

---

[39] This move was taught to me by Felina Rakowski-Gallegher, the owner of The Upper Breast Side. I mentioned this place earlier. You can find out more in the Resources section. *See also*: the scene of (one of) my meltdown(s).

4. The Milkshake[40]

Turn your hands so the palms face towards you. Place the center of your palms directly over your nipples, your fingers pointing *either* toward one another *or* towards your face. Then shake. Gently. But with fervor!

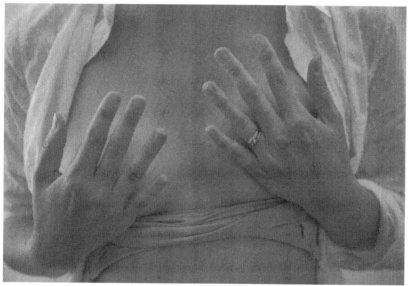

The Milkshake

---

[40] Yes, I know what song is in your head right now. Yes, it's in mine too, and the minds of the clients I see when I go on lactation visits with my mentor, Andrea. Andrea is also the person who taught me this one, so she gets the credit. (And in case it's not in your schema, especially since many of you don't live in the US, the song is called "Milkshake;" it's sung by Kelis and was released in 2003. And it will *get in your head*. Consider yourself warned.)

43

5. Kneading

Make your C-shape with two hands on one breast. Move your hands down in a kneading motion, allowing your thumbs to take the lead on the kneading.

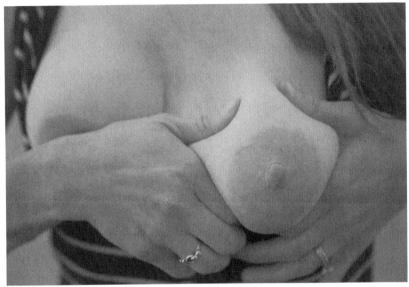

Kneading

6. Wild Card

There are so many other ways to massage one's breasts. Just among our team of MilkinMamas, we have teachers who use a light stroking touch with their fingertips to encourage the milk to let down, relying solely on oxytocin; some who lean over and give their breasts a little shake or use gentle (or not-so-gentle) slapping motions; and others who use two flat hands moving parallel to each other to jostle things up in there. We're big fans of any and all motions that move toward the nipple, because they support that feeling of "I'm getting my milk out!" That said, other motions (not necessarily toward the nipple) can work great, too. Play around and find what works best for you.

How Not to Massage
1. Any way that hurts.
2. Any way that strains your body (bruises, chafed skin, pain when you're not expressing).
3. Any way makes you feel bad (stressed, anxious, frustrated, disappointed, sad, not-enough).

FAQs about Massage:

How long should I massage?
You should massage until you're done. "Done" can mean a number of things: milk is starting to come out, you're bored, your body just says, "I'm done with this now." If you *really* need a number: 30-60 seconds is a good amount of time to massage before compressing, though I sometimes spend longer, especially if the massage is feeling really good and productive.

How much pressure should I use?
Use enough pressure to get the milk out, but not so much that it causes any pain,[41] bruising, or chafing of the skin. How's that for an exact science?

Am I using one hand or two?
You know the answer, don't you? *You get to decide!* And also: you can do some of both. Massage with one hand or two, with the right hand on the right breast or the left breast, and vice versa, all around.

---

[41] If you are already experiencing pain from clogged ducts, engorgement, or any other situation, it's tough to avoid pain altogether. As with everything, find the balance that works for you.

Can I massage one breast with the opposite hand?

Yes, and you should. Using my right hand on my left breast activates different ducts than using my left hand. I switch hands and breasts often, both for massage and compression. Variety is the spice of life, and of milking yourself.

What if it hurts?

Do you have a lactation support professional yet? If not, now is the time to find a fantastic one who can offer you consistent help, in-person and otherwise, individually and in support groups. It's important to find the cause of the pain, and a trained professional can help you do this.[42]

If you have any questions beyond what's listed here, check out the FAQs and Resources sections towards the end of this book, and reach out to us anytime. Remember, **you are never alone!**

Compression: Everything You Need to Know

Now that we've talked a lot about massage, let's discuss compression: the remaining 49% of this practice. Compression means putting pressure on the breast or chest tissue to help the milk come out, and that pressure is what differentiates these motions from the massage techniques. Pressure is what gets the milk out.

---

[42] If you can't find someone local to you, we may have a teacher at TheMilkinMama who can help. At the time of this writing, we have teachers in 10 areas of the US, plus availability for virtual support. See the Resources section later in this book to find someone who's a great match for you.

As you learn compression, remember that it's really important to be gentle. Compression should almost never hurt.[43]

I'll tell a short story to illustrate. Tell someone to "go milk yourself," and most likely you'll see them holding their breast with their fingers, and then sliding their thumb down their skin. We seem to think this is how we might milk a cow or other lactating mammal if we visited or worked on a farm.[44] When I hand expressed in my "trial by fire" experience on that yoga retreat, I left with bruise-like shadows on the tops of my breasts, all from pressing too hard using the "slide my thumb" method. The pressure was too intense, causing friction as I went, and that led to chafing that took months to go away.

With any technique, remember: compression in and of itself should not hurt. It should not cause damage, visible or otherwise. If you find you need lubrication to support your compression practice and prevent chafing, consider using a pure oil to lubricate your skin so you avoid what happened to me. (Coconut oil is my favorite for this.)

---

[43] Compression sometimes *does* hurt, as tender breasts do happen, especially in the early days of breastfeeding. If your breasts are already painful or sore, *and* you need to hand express, you may experience discomfort. Any which way, if you are experiencing *any* pain during or between feedings, please find an awesome lactation professional to help you.
[44] Clients and friends who grew up milking animals on farms tell me otherwise. The motion is less a pulling, tugging, or sliding; and more about mindful placement of the hands, followed by gentle pressure.

Select Methods for Compression

The four main compression techniques we teach at TheMilkinMama are listed here, and as always, I encourage you to play until you find what works for you.

1. Open and Close

Make a C-shape on one breast, using one or two hands. Narrow your C to compress your thumb and four fingers into your breast. Then release your fingers and thumb to open your C. This should be a quick compression motion, almost as if the parts of your hand are bouncing on the breast. Repeat. Move around and repeat. Repeat.

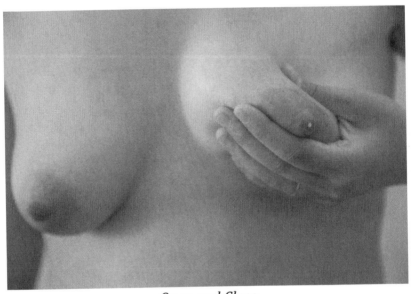

Open and Close

2. Rolling Your Thumb

With your hand in a C-shape, roll your thumb on your breast like you would for a thumbprint, from one edge to the other.

Try this with your thumb on or close to your areola, and farther back, to find the spot that helps get the milk out.

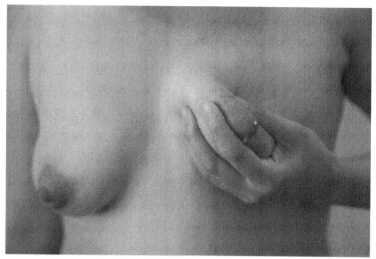

Rolling Your Thumb

3. Slide Your Thumb

This is what most people envision when they hear "go milk yourself." You *can* move your thumb along your skin in a repetitive, short, sliding motion, while compressing, much like my kids slide their ice pops up the little plastic sleeves to reach their mouths, but be gentle. Your other fingers will rest comfortably or move as needed to support the milk that's flowing into your vessel.

In our curriculum materials for teachers and birth workers, this move is listed alongside an image of a flag—*Warning!*— as it's the compression move most likely to cause discomfort/pain if done too forcefully. If using this method, consider lubricating the skin of your breast or chest before sliding your thumb.

FRANCIE WEBB

4. Press and Hold

In short: press one spot with a finger or multiple fingers. Brace the rest of the breast comfortably as you do this. Hold as long as the spray, stream, or drip keeps going. Repeat as you like.

I use this move when I have a spot that's extra full. For example, when I'm away from baby for an extended period of time and I'm trying my darnedest not to get clogged ducts (because they are the WORST), I'll go to the area where my milk likes to hang out, find the fullest spot, hold my breast with my C-shape, and press into that full spot with my thumb. Sometimes, milk will come streaming out from the pressure on that duct, and I'll hold pressure on that point until the flow stops.

Another approach is using a different finger to apply pressure. One of our Go Milk Yourself teachers showed me a Press and Hold move where she braced the bottom of her breast with her C-shape, lifted her index finger, and gently pressed it on a spot where she felt full. The stream that resulted had the strength of the Super Soaker water guns that were popular all summer when I was a kid. It was so badass, and yet so gentle. She could compress gently and easily, to great effect, because she knew where the milk was, and because she'd done some gentle stroking of that area before she pressed.

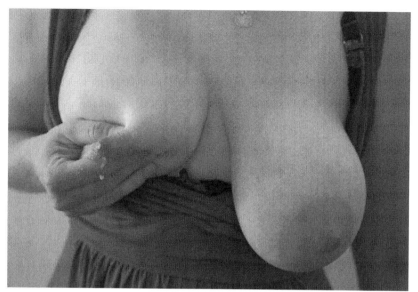

Press and Hold

5. Wild Card

Just like massage, there are so many ways to compress. One of our clients, who knew hand expression quite well already before she came to us, slides her thumbs on both breasts while leaning over a mixing bowl, and milkfalls come pouring out. That works great for her. With practice, you too will find what works for you.

FRANCIE WEBB

Specialty Tools

Some tools we teach are both massage-y and compression-y. Note that these are not called "advanced" tools – you can do them even if you're a Go Milk Yourself newborn, just unfurling into the world of hand expression.

1. Clearing the Pathway

I learned this technique during my first bout with clogged ducts, which let me tell you, was nearly as painful as childbirth.[45] This is great for when there is clogged duct, mastitis, or any hard or fuller spot in the breast.

Take one, two or three[46] fingers together, matching the width of your combined fingers to the width of the clog / hard spot. Put your finger(s) directly in FRONT of the spot, between it and the nipple. Massage in small circles from the spot to the nipple. Then, place your finger(s) behind the spot, closer to the breastbone. Now, with that same small circular motion, move down, massaging through the spot and all the way to the nipple again. After a few rounds of massaging in these two sections, try whatever your favorite compression

---

[45] For those of you who don't know, clogged ducts means that milk get stuck and can't come out. Mastitis is when the breast or chest tissue gets inflamed, either due to an infection and/or due to milk stasis. And as for this technique, Andrea Syms-Brown taught me this one, too. It really saved my boobs at the time, and it continues to do the same even when I'm not clogged!

[46] If you have to use four fingers because the mass is so wide, or these problems happen often, please find a fantastic lactation professional to help you in healing, determining the root cause of your challenges, and developing a plan to move forward.

technique is. (Mine is the Open and Close.) Repeat this whole process as needed.

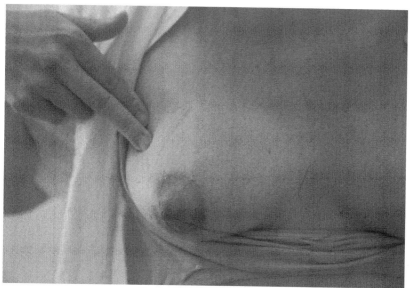

Clearing the Pathway

2. Slide and Press

This is a tool that integrates massage and compression in a slow, steady movement. If you feel that a particular line along your breast is extra full, make a C-shape at the back of your breast. Then slide your C down that full area in a line, with the fullest part in the space behind your top knuckles, applying pressure with your fingers the entire time you are sliding. This may help you get a steady stream or an increased number of streams and drips.

Slide and Press

Try following your Slide and Press with the Press and Hold or the Open and Close. See how that goes for you!

3. Two Hands

As I've mentioned, some parents find that using two hands to express yields more milk at once. This works well if your breasts are, let's say, more than one handful. You can use two hands with any move you'd like. If you wanted to use my favorite combo, C-shape + Open and Close, make two C-shapes with your hands on either side of your breast. Place a bottle or bowl in front of and below you either on a table, counter, ottoman, or even between your knees. Lean over the bottle or bowl, pointing your nipple towards and into it. Even while you're leaning, aim to keep your shoulders back and down to avoid scrunching them towards your ears. Check your comfort, as you would with all compressions. I know a mother who used two hands, one on each breast, and made this work for her for nearly a year after her daughter stopped latching and she decided to exclusively hand express. It can be done, and it's really something to see!

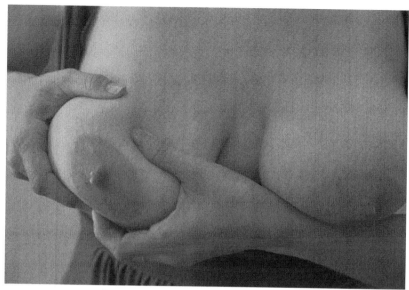

Two Hands

Move Like You: Integrating Massage and Compression
One of my favorite lines from a favorite yoga teacher is "Move like you." They'll say it after they've instructed the class through a series of poses. "Move like you" means: now that you've learned the basic structure of this series, adjust it however you need so that it feels awesome inside *your* body. So that you get exactly what you need.

Similarly, when you Go Milk Yourself, **move like you**. Make it yours.

Play around with different techniques and combinations of techniques. Dabble in the different tools you've learned to discover which ones are consistently comfortable and effective for you. Allow your practice to evolve naturally as you go, and if something stops working for you, it's okay!

There is no Right way to do this, and you can remind your self of that anytime you need to make an adjustment to your practice.

Through all this, keep in mind: yoga isn't only about the poses, and compression isn't only about squeezing your boobs. Just as it's important to integrate breath into a yoga flow, it's important to integrate massage into hand expression. (Just as my first client learned to do, after she texted me about how long it was taking her to hand express!)

If you're not sure where to start in terms of integrating massage and compression, here are some things you can do to move like you:

1. Stop compressing every so often and massage.[47]
2. Alternate breasts rather than "finishing" with one before moving to the other.
3. Alternate hands on each breast to reach all ducts.[48]
4. Continue to guess and check, using all the sensory information you discover to lead the way.

As you improve your practice, you'll make adjustments *all the time*. Even when you've become a MilkinMaster! Stay open, and your milk ducts will too!

In learning hand expression, or any other practice, notice if you're pushing or forcing. This often happens when we start to get frustrated, because we want our milk, and our lives, to

---

[47] As I mentioned before, this is a great thing to do when the flow stops, slows, or goes away altogether.
[48] Follow right hand on right breast with left hand on right breast, and the opposite for the other side. Switch sides and hands often. This will also help keep your hands from getting too tired. As will mindful alignment and posture!

flow. If the moves we make in hopes of supporting ourselves are actually adding more stress, then we're undermining our own enoughness. It's important to be able to recognize when you need to take a break, walk away from something, and come back in a different headspace.

Bottom line, as always: **You get to decide.**

(I'll be abbreviating that as **YGTD** from here on out, so stay with me.)

And if you need support, reach out. **You are never alone.**

So You Think You Can't Hand Express
In the process of learning to Go Milk Yourself, you will probably feel convinced, at least once, that you can't do it. That's totally okay. And also, it's not true. You CAN do it.

Most of us have been taught to believe, whether intentionally or unintentionally, that we cannot do the things that we *think* we cannot do. We allow our thoughts and fears (*I seriously doubt I can do this*) to take root as Truth (*I can't do this*).

The truth is: in learning most new skills, hand expression definitely included, we encounter challenges, and there usually is at least one moment when that fear creeps in. Not-enoughness. But with practice, we can overcome these challenges. In hand expression and in life.

The truth is: you're going to have to let go of limiting beliefs[49] such as "I can't do this." If you're going to master hand expression (or anything else), you'll have to stop accepting

---

[49] In case you're not familiar with the term, a limiting belief is a false belief that we develop that keeps us from doing something we truly want to do. It's a *belief* that *limits* us!

negative thoughts as Truth and start believing in the thoughts that really work for you.

The truth is: you know your body best. And when it comes to hand expression, it's best to let your body lead the way.

The truth is: you'll have to practice.

The truth is: You Can Do This.

The truth is: **You are enough**. In hand expression and in life.

See! There are a lot of different truths out there. And they can all be true, at the same time! This goes back to the idea that there isn't one Right way to do any one thing, and also, the truth is that **you get to decide** what's true for you, and I get to speak my truth about my faith in you!

Even with all that truth, there are a few limiting beliefs that routinely come up when people are considering if hand expression is going to work for them.

Let's name those now.

Limiting Belief: I can't. It'll make my wrists/thumb/fingers hurt. And/or, "I have carpal tunnel."

Truth: Hi! Your friendly author, Francie, here! You can't see me, but I'm waving at you with *both* hands. I'm a longtime sufferer of carpal tunnel syndrome (diagnosed at age 9), so believe me when I say, *I hear you.*

Repetitive stress injuries, including carpal tunnel, are a thing. So are joint issues related to pregnancy, childbirth, and holding, feeding, and schlepping babies.

That said, there are many, many ways to prevent fatigue and pain in your hands, wrists, and fingers while hand expressing. If you're open to playing around (rather than letting your (real or hypothetical) injury bench you from the get-go), you'll likely find something that works for you. In the meantime:

a.   Check your posture. Sit comfortably, with everything from your neck to the tips of your fingers as relaxed as possible.[50]

b.   Keep your shoulders and elbows down; if you notice that you are hiking shoulders or elbows up to get into Go Milk Yourself position, make a change. Re-relax. Release your body so you can release your milk.

c.   Keep your joints as aligned as possible. No tweaking of the wrists (twerking is totally fine, if you're that talented and into it). No curling or clenching of the fingers. Just. Be.

d.   Use *just enough* pressure to get the milk out. Using more pressure than needed causes strain.

e.   Switch hands and breasts often. Take breaks whenever you need to.

Limiting Belief: I can't. My breasts are too small / large / floppy / imperfect in some other way.

Truth: If you have hands and breasts with milk in them, and if you are anywhere from slightly curious about hand

---

[50] If you need more support, re-read the section about posture and relaxing, which you'll find in the Hand Expression Basics section in Chapter 5.

expression to downright determined to make it work for you, you can hand express.[51]

The perfection of your breasts is never in question, and with the exception of true primary lactation failure, there is no breast I've met yet that truly couldn't be hand expressed. (And I've met lots of boobs.)

Remember: Your body is AMAZING. **You are enough**!

Limiting Belief: I can't. I have implants or have had breast augmentation surgery.

Truth: If you have implants or have had any kind of breast surgery, you may be able to hand express. The deciding

---

[51] There is a massive caveat here, and I want to address it out of respect for all parents who have suffered from this. Primary lactation failure, when a parent's body is physiologically unable to make milk for their baby, can be caused by having insufficient glandular tissue (IGT) within the breast or chest. It can also result from hormonal postpartum issues like retained placenta or thyroid problems. Finally, sometimes milk production doesn't happen because breastfeeding wasn't established well in the beginning due to situations such as separation of parent and baby, not removing milk often enough, or baby having problems transferring milk. These circumstances are often challenging and sometimes devastating. For the rest of this section, and the majority of this book, I'll be operating under the assumption that lactation failure is not the case for the people I'm addressing. And if you have been through it, I send you my love, and I hope you can get some beautiful lessons from this book nonetheless.

factors are whether you are able to produce milk (which depends on the specific procedures done during your surgery), and whether you (and your medical provider / others on your team) deem it safe for you.

The same applies as above: if you have hands, boobs, and milk, you can hand express.

Limiting Belief: I can't. I've never done it before. I don't know how.

Truth: I mean, me neither! But then I did. And it worked! Sully (you know, the pilot who landed a plane on the Hudson River a few years back) said, "Everything is unprecedented until it happens for the first time." And he's one of my heroes.[52]

I *could* sit here and make a list of all the things I've done in my life that I'd never done before I...you know...did them. It would be a LONG list.

If you're currently stuck in this fear about not knowing how, I suggest you make a list of all the things you didn't know how to do at some point that you now do regularly. Empower yourself to try something new by taking stock of the times you have *done the impossible.* Because there are many. (If you're ready to actually make this list right now and want some further support, turn to The Most Important Person section in Chapter 6 for a bit more guidance.)

---

[52] If you haven't watched the movie *Sully*, please, please go watch it. If you are a crier like me, bring your tissues. It's one of those films I could watch over and over again, every time I need a pick-me-up, and it would very much pick me up. A must-see.

FRANCIE WEBB

Limiting Belief: I can't. I tried. It didn't work.

Truth: I KNOW THE FEELING. That's how it goes sometimes, right? When I first tried to hand express, it didn't work for me either. I got a few sprays in the shower and then it stopped. I didn't think much of it, and when, a few months later, a woman at a breastfeeding group mentioned hand expressing into a bottle for her baby, I still felt a sense of awe and "I could never do that!"

But you know what? I tried again later. Repeatedly. And eventually, it worked for me. And now it works beautifully!

I won't tell you "If at first you don't succeed, try, try again." But I will tell you that if you want this to work for you, and if you follow the strategies in this book, and if you reach out for help in whatever ways feel right to you, you will likely find that the result is worth the effort.

Bottom Line: You CAN do things you think you *cannot* do. That includes practicing the badass art of hand expression.

Keyword there? *Practice.* **With practice, you have power, and it's all in your hands.**

Once you start practicing regularly, everything will be perfect. All your problems will be solved, and you'll live a perfect life, forevermore. Hand expression, and everything else, will be a breeze.

PSYCH.

That was a lie. Again. (Sometimes I lie to make a point.)

The truth is: most of us encounter challenges when we first start hand expressing. Matter of fact, most of us encounter challenges when we first try to learn *anything* new. But with practice (and troubleshooting!), we can overcome these challenges.

Troubleshooting

In this section, I'll share some of the most common challenges that come up during hand expression, and I'll offer some ideas for getting through, past, or over them— whatever suits your badass fancy. And remember, even if these things don't work right at first, you'll discover what does as you continue to *move like you* and to deepen into your own practice.

Challenge: I only get drips and drops.

What to Do: Keep practicing. Try different positions, different hands, more massage, alternating breasts. Play with the timing and get creative if you need to: some parents stop their pumping session early and hand express after, with great results. Reach out to TheMilkinMama for help, anytime. **You are never alone.**

Challenge: My hand/lap/whole life is covered in milk.

What to Do: First, GO YOU. Loooooooooooook at all that milk!!! Second, don't stress about losing liquid gold—**there's more where that came from**. Third, to manage the milk-everywhere sitch:

> 1. Try a position switch. Bending at the waist (still keeping your shoulders back and down as your torso tilts forward) can make a big difference, since you can aim directly down into the vessel.

2. Grab a wider vessel. Mug, glass measuring cup, and mixing bowl are all solid options. The bottle with pump setup—breastshield and all—works great too.

3. As Elsa would say, "Let it go, let it goooooooooo . . ." (definitely can't hold that milk back anymoooooooore!) It's awesome that you're hand expressing so well. Use that sticky hand to pat yourself on the back!

Challenge: It hurts. A lot.

What to Do: Seek help, first and foremost. Pain is a sign that something is awry. A fantastic local lactation professional can guide you. Consult your medical provider(s) and other experts in your life as you see fit. Book a session with a MilkinMama teacher. If you must express while in pain, be as gentle as you can.

Challenge: My hand/wrist/thumb is sore.

What to Do: First, stop. Stretch, shake out your hands, relax. When you try again, check your positioning, ensuring that everything from your neck to your fingers is as relaxed and aligned as possible.

Take breaks when you need to, both during hand expression and throughout your day when you notice tension in the body. Try yoga, stretching, and being mindful of your alignment (for example, not twisting your wrist or clenching your fingers) in everyday tasks, such as carrying baby. Consider reaching out to a professional, like a physical therapist, if these tricks don't help.

Challenge: Nothing comes out.

What to Do: If you haven't been at it very long, keep practicing. Reread the book and set an intention to discover new information this second time around. Visit the website and check out some videos to see if that inspires you in a new way. Send us an email at info@themilkinmama.com; we'll set up a time to chat and see how we can best support you.

Challenge: Nothing comes out. Ever. And I've tried a million times (*and* I've used all the resources you mentioned in the last question).

What to Do: Do you have a fantastic lactation professional? Someone who can see you live and in-person, will follow up with you, and (ideally) has a support group you can join for camaraderie in the long run? If so, YAY. If not, time to find one. Refer to our Resources section to help you find the right person for you.

Challenge: Nothing's coming out, and this has always worked before.

What to Do: First, massage and try again. Dabble in all the moves you know, including the ones that don't usually work. If something's feeling off in your body, you may need to switch up how you've been doing things. If your breasts are so hard you can't get milk out, Google *reverse pressure softening* and see if it's helpful.

Now, if these tools don't help, it's time to call the fantastic professional you already have, or it's time to find one. To connect with a new expert, check out our Resources section.

FRANCIE WEBB

Congratulations! If you've read this chapter, you now have everything you need to know to cultivate a powerful practice of hand expression in your life!

Keep in mind that you can always refer back to this section when you need support, or turn to the FAQ section for further guidance. For more interactive support, you can visit us at www.themilkinmama.com, and/or email us at info@themilkinmama. com.

In the next chapter, I'm going to get deeper into the universal life lessons I've learned on my hand expression journey, which I now am called to teach. I'll talk more about what it means to be enough, share more about my own Journey to Enoughness, and offer some advice on finding your own path to Enoughness, no matter how not-enough you're feeling right now.

If you're interested in that, read on! If not, good luck in your hand expression adventures, and see you later! Remember, *move like you.*

Chapter 6:
The Journey to Enoughness

For me, another way to think about the Journey to Enoughness is to consider it as the journey from inauthenticity to authenticity. "Authenticity" is a word that gets tossed around a lot these days, so before we go any further I'd like to share what that word means to me.

If I am coming from a place of authenticity, I'm being straight up with you. Even more important, I'm being straight up with myself. I'm making it a priority to be totally myself in every moment. And when I'm not feeling quite myself, for whatever reason, I'm making it a priority to own that feeling by acknowledging it and choosing to make a shift. Living in authenticity requires me to be vulnerabrave, especially when I'm facing a brand new challenge, which is fairly often, because living authentically is challenging.

In authenticity, you're often wearing your heart on your sleeve (pretty much the definition of vulnerabravery); and you're also learning, through trial and error, the level of discernment it takes to state your needs and boundaries clearly, and then to stick to them. You're learning to support yourself in having your needs met, and when you know your needs will be met—because you are living authentically, expressing your truth, and using your own power to ensure that you are being taken care of—you feel safe. You're able to be the most loving you can be, to yourself and others.

How does it feel to live this way? Sometimes, it feels great. In moments of powerful authenticity, when I'm living mindfully, it's as though my head, heart, and mouth are totally connected. Operating as one. The words that come out of my mouth are the same words that my heart would say, if it could speak directly; the same words that my head would say, if it had a mouth (which it kinda does—ha!).

And sometimes, it doesn't feel so great. When we're living authentically, we're often being called to act outside of our comfort zone as we let go of limiting beliefs and begin claiming our own enoughness. Many of us have gotten so used to pleasing others, to being everyone's helper, or to inhabiting a certain persona, that it can be really freaking hard to let go of what's not real and begin living from what is.

One of my beautiful internet friends,[53] Lauren Perrault, recently wrote, "The journey from inauthenticity to authenticity hurts, tears you up in a million shreds, pulls the rug, the floor, the foundation, and the earth it's sitting on from underneath you, makes you feel like you're floating out in space. But that's the journey."

Lauren's words absolutely speak to what has happened for me. They speak to how I have experienced my own journey, this shift from inauthenticity to authenticity. They speak to my experience, not just in the past few years as I've become a mother, built a business, and mastered hand expression (and my emotions, for the most part), but also throughout my entire life, the last three and a half decades in which I've ridden the rollercoaster of life.

As you Journey to Enoughness, be prepared: to feel things you've felt before and thought you were done feeling; to feel

---

[53] You have some of these, right? You'd call them "friend," but you've never actually met in person. You know a *ton* about each other and have followed and respected one another's journeys for a while now...which in internet time might actually be only a few weeks. You feel like real friends. You know what I'm talking about.

things you've never felt before and never imagined you would; and to go through both kinds of experiences over and over and over.

For me, this often sounds like:

What is this feeling? It feels icky, yet familiar. Oh, that's right, this is what it feels like when I think I'm not enough. But I now know the truth: I am enough. I used to feel like this all the time. Like I was living in struggle, and no matter what I did, I couldn't escape. The struggle was constant. A way of being. That's not who I am anymore. Ugh, I thought I was done with this! What do I need right now? I can tell by the way I'm feeling that I'm in need of a shift. What can I let go of here? How can I support myself through this? I've got this!!!

I know I've got this, because I've been practicing, and because I've been through this over and over and over now. This is a massive new concept in my life: that if you're *really living*, expanding into the most authentic version of your awesome self, there's a good chance it's going to be *crazy* challenging. But the truth is: you're never done. Not until you're dead. The lessons keep coming and coming, challenging you to find deeper and deeper reservoirs of enoughness. And, you are *always* enough.

In other words, the journey never ends. (At least not until it's like OVER.) This is where committed practice comes in. With practice, we have the tools to find our way back to Enoughness anytime we take a not-enough detour. To illustrate, here's a story:

Not too long ago, I was having a very messy mom morning. We'd just returned from visiting my in-laws on the west coast, my big girl and I were still operating three hours behind, ready to sleep all morning, but baby sister[54] was wiiiiiide awake, first thing. Schools were closed mid-week for a holiday, so to get some work done, I had to schlep the two children to two different locations for the day. Despite one of them being tired, the girls were in great moods. I was the one wearing my crankypants.

After stopping at Dunkin Donuts for a corn muffin breakfast (#momoftheyear), we braved the wild that is the NYC commute, always made wilder by adding kiddos. In the cab I hailed because it was one of *those* mornings, my big girl spilled corn muffin crumbs all over while, in one of the *five* bags I was carrying, a bottle of milk spilled silently, a white puddle spreading over the cab floor.

When I saw the puddle of milk, I heard in my head:

"You are a *disaster*."

And there it was. Not-enoughness. Right there in my own self-talk. An old, practiced habit—words at the ready to respond to the normal shenanigans of having young kids, words reflecting my not-enoughness—internalized so deeply and so well.

I felt a pang. That old familiar feeling in the body. I. Am Not. Enough. And I never will be. Confirmation of the Truth.

And yet, not the truth at all.

Thankfully, having been on this ride a time or two (million), I know how to handle this kind of unexpected detour to Not Enough. I've practiced. I took a deep breath and, amidst the

---

[54] My big girl went through a phase where she called her sister "Bae Sister." How cute is that?!

peals of kids' laughter as they poked each other, and the cab driver's assurances that it was okay, he could clean up the milk, I flipped the script.

"Nope. Francie: You are *not* a disaster. The milk spilled. There are crumbs in the car. You're running late and feeling frazzled today. Those are facts. But *you* are NOT a disaster. You are a HUMAN. And a damn good one, at that."

In that moment, I made a choice to release the judgment and deepen into the truth of my enoughness.

If you're going to commit to the Journey to Enoughness, sooner or later, you're going to have to release judgment, and you're going to have to practice. Because my friends!!! We judge ourselves ALL THE TIME.

For me, it sounds like:

"Dammit Frances."[55]
"You've got to be kidding me."
"What is my name?"[56]
"You've got to stop doing this!"
"Fuck fuck fuck fuck fuck."[57]

---

[55] You already know who gets to call me this.
[56] I am not lying: I say this out loud when I'm trying to remember whatever it was I was just going to do...
[57] My husband contributed this one. I asked him what I say when I'm all worked up, and he couldn't recall, or wouldn't share. Then I got upset with him for throwing away ¼ of a paper towel on which I'd written two really important sentences for this book, in Sharpie. So I said this, and he offered it back to me as contribution. (And then I found the paper towel note on my nightstand a few hours later.) (And then I didn't end up using those sentences...)

FRANCIE WEBB

"I just can't keep up."

And oh—OH!—there are so many more.

We judge ourselves all day long.

Most of us learn this behavior as kids. We learn it through messages our parents pass down, both purposefully and inadvertently. We internalize the belief that there is a Right way to live, *and* a Wrong way (which means all the ways that aren't the Right one), and thus, we walk around judging ourselves constantly to see how we measure up. For some people, this goes on for most, if not all, of their lives. What's worse: when we embody this belief, we reinforce it for everyone else around us who is living out that same belief, and also for those who are still forming their belief systems (read: kids).

My daughter, who recently turned five, had a number of challenging tantrums in the weeks following her birthday. At one point when I stopped to talk with her, when I felt we were both in a calm place, she started sobbing and through the tears said, "I'm not your best daughter anymore!" She's *already* judging herself. Worrying about disappointing me and others. *She's five.*

This cycle of judgment is heartbreaking, and it keeps us from living in our enoughness.

If we intend to begin living inside authenticity, inside all the messiness of our humanity, inside the knowledge of our enoughness, we have to let it go. We do that by flipping the script, in the moment, as the judgment is happening.

If you're new to this practice of releasing judgment, a great way to begin is by treating yourself like the most awesome person you've ever met. [58] If it helps, imagine your awesomest people: A family member. Your partner. Your child. The celebrity whose poster hung on your ceiling in your teenage years. An incredible teacher whose lessons still inspire you on the daily. Whatever works for you! **YGTD!**

You'd never approach any of those people and say, "Oh, hey, best person ever, YOU SUCK!" Instead, you'd react with love and compassion, coming to their aid. Take what you would say to that person if you witnessed them in a messy, human moment, and say it to yourself instead.

It might sound like:

- You've got this.
- You can do *anything!*
- I admire you.
- I appreciate you.
- Your work has changed my life.
- You're totally making my day—no, my life.
- You're doing great.
- It is such an honor to be (with) you.
- You're. So. Awesome.
- **You are enough!**

Chaos is a given in life. And it's definitely a given on the Journey to Enoughness.

Regardless of where you're at on your journey, There will be a whole lotta chaos as you go from little old you to *truly, madly, deeply*[59] you. But if you're committed, you're going to

---

[58] Author Jen Sincero taught me this concept. She's in the Resources section.
[59] You know that song, right? I love '90s music!

realize that *you actually do have power, **especially** when you think you don't.*[60]

Your saving grace in the midst of this chaos?

You Get to Decide.
This concept has already come up a lot in this book, I know. That's because, when we talk about creating a committed practice of authenticity, it really comes down to grounding into and living out two essential truths: **you get to decide** and **you are the most important person.**

I've learned the importance of **YGTD** most directly from working in the birth world, because as a doula, I empower people to trust themselves and to decide for themselves. I support expectant and new parents in making choices that feel good to them, telling them all the time: **You get to decide** what you do and don't feel comfortable with, because **you are the most important person**.

In empowering others to make choices that feel good, and witnessing the growth that occurs when people begin trusting themselves enough to act like they are the most important person(s), I've also learned how to empower myself. How to lead by example and act, in my own life, like I am the most important person.

---

[60] Maybe *especially* then. Because that's when you're most vulnerable, and within your vulnerability lies your power. I'm a big, big fan of vulnerability. It gives you impetus to dig in, go inside your self, to figure out who you really are and what you want. And there, you'll find your power. Sometimes, it is when we're at our most lost that we can see ourselves, and what we need the most, clearly.

It wasn't always this way. When I was a neophyte at motherhood—my first child growing inside me—my doula told me something I will never forget:

"You Are the Most Important Person."
I was like, "WHAT. IS. SHE. TALKING. ABOUT."

I don't think I even said anything in response. The whole concept confused me thoroughly, and it wasn't until much later that I began to understand the meaning of her words.

We hired Karla, our beloved doula, at a time when I felt quite anxious, and *definitely* not-enough. I was moving through a lot, emotionally.[61] At my 20-week anatomy scan (a common ultrasound used to check out all of baby's parts and see how things are growing in there), the doctor told me that my baby was "measuring small." In other words, her body parts were measuring smaller than expected for the age she was in the womb. The doctor said I didn't need to do anything differently, but recommended I come back in three weeks for another check.

At the 23-week mark, I headed to the hospital's maternal and fetal medicine unit for what we came to know as "growth scans." Shortly after beginning, the ultrasound technician told me she needed to call for the doctor (which we all know is *never* a good sign), and in walked an older man whose face I don't even remember. Though I do remember how awful he made me feel.

---

[61] I feel confident that *all* expectant parents (and most people, honestly) are moving through a lot, emotionally! (That's kind of what it means to be alive!)

FRANCIE WEBB

This man wasn't my doctor; he was a high-risk doctor based at the hospital, only called in if the technician noticed something wrong or unusual on the ultrasound screen. "Your baby is too small," he said. "We're going to put you on bed rest. You don't need to be working anyway." This comment enraged me. Who was he to say whether I should or should not be working? What did he know of my work, which I'd loved for many years and dedicated so much of myself to? And what year was this?! I felt the weight of patriarchal condescension.

In shock, (and thinking anxiously about the 80 middle-school students and 9 teachers who were waiting for me to join them on that day's field trip, which I'd organized singlehandedly and was also meant to lead), I asked a few questions. I was hoping to talk him out of his prescription so I could continue living my normal life.

I didn't get very far.

"We're going to need to do some further monitoring. We'll need you to come back for regular scans. I'm concerned about trans-placental…" He drifted off into medicalese.

By now, I was sobbing. With tears streaming down my face and fear in my heart, I'd given up all thoughts of the field trip. *Something was wrong with my baby.* It *had* to be my fault. Right?! Whose else could it be? What had I done wrong?! As I spun out internally, he continued on his tangent.

I broke in again, still crying, barely able to get the words out. "Excuse me. I was pre-med, and I *still* don't understand what you're saying. I need you to talk to me like I'm a human being and not a textbook." Something in my tone must have caught his attention, because he looked down at me, surprise in his eyes, seemingly noticing for the first time that his words were upsetting me.

"Oh. I mean, we have to see if there's something wrong with your placenta that would mean that the baby's not getting enough nutrients."

Something wrong with your placenta.

Something wrong with you.

You. Are Not. Enough.

This is what I heard.

I can't for the life of me remember what happened next, but I do remember calling my own OBGYN after I left and leaving a message with her office through my tears. Then my husband and my fragile self headed to a favorite diner to eat a massive meal, in hopes that food (nutrients!) would help the baby. I had to do *something*. Even as we ate, I marinated in my not-enoughness.

It was my fault. I was not enough, and my baby was suffering because of it.

My doctor called me back an hour later. "I was one floor away at the hospital, and they know you're my patient. They should have called me!" She sounded furious at how I'd been treated. She told me that bed rest wasn't totally necessary; we'd try two weeks of "house rest" instead. I came to call this "house (ar)rest", because it was a modified bed rest situation in which I could do whatever I wanted, but I was only to leave the house *very* occasionally for a *very* good reason.[62] And always with an escort, of course.

And so began nearly four months—almost half my pregnancy—of restricted activity. I spent seven weeks at home, worrying and watching "Say Yes to the Dress," wracked with guilt about not being at school. I also slept a lot, and after many years of working insane hours, it was actually nice to have a break. And to be honest, the escort part was pretty great too, because when I did want to go somewhere, **I was never alone**, and that helped remind me how supported I was, am, and ever shall be!

Even though the break was needed, I itched to get back to my normal life. Week after week, I asked my doctor, "What do you need to see in order for me to be able to go back to work?" She finally agreed that as long as baby showed consistent growth, I could go back—with reduced hours and a list of restrictions, including an order to take cabs back and forth to school.

On top of everything else, I got a phone call about 5 weeks before my due date that crushed my hopes of giving birth in my hospital's birth center. My doctor wanted to monitor the baby more closely during my labor than the birth center was equipped for, and although baby's measurements were out of the zone considered "dangerous," she was still smaller than average. I was disappointed, but my doctor, whom I'd loved

---

[62] My doctor defined a reason as "*very* good" if I had to go see her, go to the hospital for monitoring, and do anything that qualified as relaxation or self-care, like a brunch with a friend or a massage. I was definitely on board with these last couple of "very good reasons" to leave the house. Very good, indeed!

and trusted for over a decade, wanted to "err on the safe side."

It was tough.

Enter Karla: the silver lining through all this. We hired a doula partially because I needed someone to talk me out of all the worry—the thoughts of not-enoughness that were coming up for me day in and day out. Someone to tell me my baby was okay. That I was okay. Over and over again.

So one day Karla says it: **"You are the most important person."**

If I'm remembering correctly, she said it in the context of me feeling torn between my two worlds and my two loves—my love for work and my desire to do whatever it took to make sure my baby was okay. And as I've mentioned, when she said it, I had no clue what she was talking about.

As I sat at home, incubating my child, knowing others were teaching my students at school, wishing that things were different and that I could get back to my *life*, I slowly but surely began to learn what Karla meant: that taking care of myself as if **I am the most important person**, benefits everyone.

After a few more years of sitting with this concept, I've come to understand it more fully. Now, I *know* that:

1. I am important. Straight up.
2. I deserve to care for myself, and to be cared for by others.
3. I deserve care just as much as all the people I always care for, *including my own children*, deserve it.
4. When I put myself first, everybody wins.

With the support of Karla, and so many other people, I got through that first pregnancy. I had a beautiful, healthy baby who weighed 6 lbs 10 oz, and while I don't necessarily think that the house (ar)rest prescription is what kept my baby healthy,[63] it did teach me to slow down, to just be, to gather a team to support me, to seek out and accept help, and to *rest*. To treat myself as **the most important person.** And all those lessons have served me, and continue to serve me and all those I care for, to this day.

Bottom Line: The most important thing to know as you begin practicing **YGTD** is that **you are the most important person.** Because when you do things that make you feel good (that make you feel *important*...like you *matter*), you feel good. And you treat others better, because you feel good, and that supports you in being good to others.

I know what you might be thinking:

That's cute. And utterly impossible. I'm a MOM / DAD/ PARENT / BUSY PERSON. I don't have time to take a bath / plan a vacation / switch the Pandora from Disney to my favorite classical guitarist / get back on my bike after so many years off / find a new doctor because this one isn't doing it for me.

Or:

It just makes life easier to do whatever the nearest expert tells me to do. I don't have the energy to talk to my doctor about

---

[63] I now know the doctors were being overly cautious, so much so, that I chose not to work with them for my next pregnancy, despite having loved my OB since my first year out of college. And because **I get to decide** who's on my team.

concerns that I have, or to do my own research, or to find a new provider if it comes to that. I'm already giving all I can give, right now.

And to *any* and *all* of that I say: I don't care what it is; if it makes you feel good, you should do it. Soon. Sooner rather than later.

Ask yourself:

What if *I took care of myself* **at least as well** *as I cared for others? What if I took care of myself as well as I care for the most important people in my life? What would that look like? Who would benefit? How might that help me reach my dreams and serve my purpose?*

Many people shut down as soon as they're asked this kind of question.

"It's impossible."

Right?

What if, instead of pooh-poohing such ideas, you stopped to ask: *What do I really need right now?* Ask the question the same way you might if you were getting down on a child's level to discover what they need, trying to make them feel better in that moment. You'd do that for an upset or anxious child, wouldn't you? Now do it for your *self.*

Grab a Post-It, notebook, journal, back of a receipt, piece of child's artwork you snuck into the recycling bin. **Take a moment to make a list of ten things you need right now to feel good.** Big or small, it doesn't matter.

Choose one that you can do in the next 24 hours.

Schedule it into your calendar. Right now. Be specific about the start and end time. Commit to it.

Now, your job is to follow through. Do that thing. Feel good. Be glad you did. And then keep doing that.

If 24 hours feels like too much of a stretch, give yourself a week. Or a month. **You get to decide** what kind of timeline feels good to you, just as much as **you get to decide** what it is that you need. But don't chicken out here. Take the time to take care of *you*.

Act as if you deserve it. Because you *do*.

Once you understand the importance of YGTD—that is to say, once you realize that you have power, in your own life and in this world, and you can choose to use that power whenever you want—you'll have everything you need[64] to enjoy your own Journey to Enoughness, even when it is challenging.

What does "challenging" really look like? No surprise here, it looks a lot like creeping thoughts of not-enoughness:

I can't.
That'll never happen.
I wish I could, but . . .
There's a snowball's chance in hell that I could do that.

---

[64] To name a few: A strong relationship with—and love for—yourself; a thoughtfully constructed team of supporters and experts; a clear sense of what's okay and what's not okay with and for you; a willingness to meet challenges with an authentic and open heart; some experience with actively healing from past hurts; a clear idea of your purpose on this earth, including and especially the people you're meant to serve, and how.

I don't have time.
There just aren't enough hours in the day!
*Things will **never** change.*
I tried that before. It didn't work.
There's just no way.
I don't have the money.
My. Whole. Life. is one step forward, two steps back.
Every time I think I'm finally getting ahead, something comes crashing down and stops me in my tracks.
I never should have _____ .
I'm always waiting for the other shoe to drop.
I just don't have it in me to _____ .

And the like.

Regardless of how long you've been on the Journey to Enoughness, when you start thinking and feeling not-enough, it can definitely feel like what you want is impossible for you, and that can take you right back to not-enough territory. It's not a pretty place, but it sure is easy to get stuck there. In fact, some people spend their whole lives in Not Enough, painfully anchored to that "Truth," to that part of them that is determined to continue believing "I am not and will never be enough," unsure why they're feeling so burdened by life.

Want to check and see if you're stuck in Not Enough? Take a moment now to make a list of things you think are impossible for you and any not-enough thoughts that have been coming up for you lately.

(Seriously, do it now. I'll wait.)

Okay.

(Did you do it? If not, do it now.)

Now, look back over the list. What do you notice? Self-doubt, excuses, doomsday-type thinking? Whatever it is, take note of that. Take note of how you're feeling as you reflect, because that's really important too. Try not to judge yourself for feeling whatever it is you're feeling or for thinking not-enough thoughts in the first place. Simply notice, acknowledge, and then commit to letting it go.

Now, it's time to make a second list. This time, ask yourself, *What is something I thought I couldn't do that I actually then did? What are some things that I thought were impossible, that actually happened?*

Write those things down as they come to you.

If something isn't coming right away, that's okay. Stick with it. Take a deep breath, or two, or ten. Relax your body. Become quiet and still. Ask yourself the question directly: *When have I done what I believed to be impossible? What have I done that I never thought I could do until I did it?*

If you're still feeling stuck, here are some of mine to give you some ideas:

1. Rode a bike without training wheels
2. Healed from a childhood injury
3. Stopped waxing my eyebrows (I *love* my eyebrows! Just as they are!)
4. Forgiven. Period.
5. Learned to love mushrooms and onions
6. Finally, finally separated from a couple of long-term, yet toxic, romantic partners
7. Jumped off a cliff in Hawaii with zero clothes on
8. Learned to love Korean spas *and* my local YMCA locker room, where (gasp!) *people see me naked*
9. Birthed a baby on my bed all by myself

10. Started a business (Limiting Belief: "I am *not* a business person")
11. Began telling my parents, siblings, and other friends that I love and appreciate them, *without feeling awkward*

And that's just the tip of the...nipple? Eleven out of so many more than eleven.

What I'm trying to say is, what we once thought impossible *becomes* possible *when we do it*.

Never sooner.

Okay, have you made your second list?

(If not, I'll wait.)

When you're done, look back over it. What do you see?

I hope you'll see, written on that page, at least one thing you thought was impossible that was actually—you guessed it—possible. Hopefully, you'll see more than one! And if not, that's still okay. As you sit with this challenge, you may find that clarity comes, or more questions do, and either of those things are great.

Because the truth is, my friends, we are all enough. And we *do* the impossible, on the daily. All of us. The simple fact that we wake up each morning, breathe, turn towards the sun, move our bodies on land and in water, heal trauma that's lived inside our bodies for years—it's all. Just. Impossible.

Yet we do it.

FRANCIE WEBB

We marvel at other animals who carry their young on their bodies, keep them warm, jump into water to save them from drowning, intuit the needs of others, travel in herds—all when we see them behind the glass at a zoo, or on the computer or TV screen. BUT WE TOO ARE FULL OF DAMN MIRACLES EVERY SINGLE DAY. We, too, do these miraculous things as if they are normal. Because they *are*. Just by being us, we are miraculous.

Because we are enough, and our bodies do miraculous things, all day, every day.

If we are so enough, what's really going on here? Why are so many people walking around disempowered, talking about all the things that are "impossible" in life? While doing the seemingly impossible with our bodies is something each of us does day in and day out (just by virtue of being alive, in my opinion), I've found that many people still need major coaching to move out of the land of impossibility about what we are and aren't capable of as humans.

I've become particularly adept at coaching parents into the realization of possibility in their lives, by helping them understand that giving birth is an "impossible" task. It's so totally insane that we grow humans inside our bodies, and then birth them, in all the ways that we do. And then we feed them with our bodies—*we actually make food inside our bodies for the humans we've created.* And *then*, with time, they become these **real people.** With boogers and bruises and bank accounts and brilliant brains!

Does it make *any* logical sense, to any of us who believes in logic, that we, as humans, create humans? That our bodies, which are so ENOUGH even as we construct them as so "imperfect," *create, and then sustain, life?* The craziest thing is, *we* were once these tiny little babies who were all, "What

86

the heck just happened?!" when we came out of our mothers' bodies in a swift, totally shocking separation.

It's all just so "impossible."

And yet we do it. Every day.

Impossible things.

You may say, "Okay, sure, my body does 'miraculous things' and all that, but that's not *me*." The truth is: you ARE your body. Kind of. When I say that your body can and does do miraculous things, that also means that YOU do miraculous things every single damn day. Take some credit for what your body does, because it's *you* doing the things. Even when you don't have conscious control over all the pieces, something wonderful is happening right there in your very own body-home.

These things are our power. They *speak to the power that we already have and have always had* just by virtue of being alive. We perform miracles on the daily, as a matter of course. Accept that you are a miraculous human with an awesome body, having an experience that no one else can have but *you*. And don't forget:

You are enough. You can do the impossible thing. You already do.

Part of the Journey to Enoughness is as simple as recognizing this as FACT. Tell yourself over and over. Fake it 'til you make it, if you need to.

Be you. And be glad that you are. Because **you are** *always* **enough**.

FRANCIE WEBB

Chapter 7:
Milestones on the Journey

Now that we've got the basics of the journey out of the way, we're going to take a deeper look at things that can come up to derail you, and how to move through them.

When Others Treat You as if You Are Not Enough

Sometimes, other humans—including humans you trust or who you perceive as having some sort of power or authority over you—will tell you that you're not enough. They'll communicate this in all kinds of ways: through their words, with their actions, by giving you the side-eye, by talking about you behind your back, by talking about you in front of your face, by going completely silent, with condescension. There are all kinds of methods, really, for one human to project their insecurities and not-enoughness onto another. There are also infinite ways for each of us to interpret the world around us, many of which powerfully reinforce our belief that we are not enough.

The most important thing to understand around all this is:

1. When someone else treats us as though we are not enough, it is *always* a manifestation of their own unchecked not-enoughness. It's never really about us. Not ever.

2. We get to choose whether or not we recognize that as fact.

The choice we make, about whether or not to buy into the not-enough that's being sold to us, determines absolutely everything about how we move through the world.[65]

When we choose to operate as we always have, inside our default of not-enoughness, that default belief is then confirmed by our experience. Someone tosses some not-enough vibes our direction, and it's not as if they are teaching or telling us something new. They are simply reaffirming our belief: We. Are Not. Enough.

What's more, once you've committed to releasing that belief and to grounding instead into the truth of your own enoughness, reflections of not-enoughness will likely start coming at you from all over the place.

So, when this happens,

Don't believe the human who seems to be confirming your not-enoughness. Recognize what's happening (an old belief is being reflected to you by someone still living in that belief system) and choose differently than you have in the past. If you choose to believe the stories of scarcity and inadequacy that come from others, you'll continue living in Not Enough. You'll integrate this "Truth" into your self-perception; you'll carry it in your body; you'll put it into your own words and repeat it in your thoughts. And then, you'll feel not-enough.

Inadequate.

Miserable.

---

[65] My favorite books that help me do this important work are Brené Brown's *Rising Strong* and Jen Sincero's *You are a Badass*. I say more about them in the Resources section.

Don't waste your time on that nonsense.

If you find yourself buying into the stories you're being told about your own not-enoughness, find a different human to believe in—yourself.

YGTD who YOU are.

You're the one living life in your body. Your heart. Your mind. No one else gets to say what's happening in there. Even when the person reflecting your not-enoughness to you seems like the Expert, **you get to decide** what's true for you.

This one time, my child's doctor made me feel very not-enough.

When my first baby was two months old, I took her to the pediatrician. We were going through *a lot* of life shenanigans at the time—think bed bugs with a newborn and the long legal fight with a landlord that followed. Needless to say, I was stressed.

The staffer whose job it was to get the basic info before the doctor arrived—I think she was a nursing assistant— weighed my little girl, then took a few other measurements. Soon after, the pediatrician, whom we'd chosen because of her popularity on a local moms' email list (at a time when I was still listening to others opinions *far more* than my own), entered the room. I'll call her Dr. G. There was no small talk. Instead, she jumped right to the issue of my girl's weight.

"She's too small. If you're open to giving her a bottle, you should do that."

I was shocked. Especially since, as you know, I'd been told that my daughter was too small throughout my *entire* pregnancy, and I had suffered through nearly two months of house (ar)rest in hopes of her growing more before arriving earthside. She'd been born at a healthy weight though, and thriving ever since, so my immediate reaction to our doctor's assertion that baby girl was too small was complete surprise.

"We both seem healthy to me."

And then,

"Of course I'm open to giving her a bottle."

Because, why not? The Expert was telling me that my baby needed a bottle. It must be true.

Knowing that milk production varies throughout the day, I asked Dr. G. when I should pump milk for the bottle. She stared. I read on her face some combination of confusion and disdain. "No. I don't mean a bottle of *breastmilk*. If you do that, I'm concerned you won't have enough milk for your baby to nurse. I meant a bottle of *formula*."

My heart fell.

Shock.

Shame.

Not-enoughness.

Truth.

(This was obviously before I learned how to flip the script when this shit happens!)

Trusting her word completely, I acquiesced. Yes, I told her, I would do that. We would go get some formula right now. She left, and I broke down sobbing.

My dear friend Rose met sobbing me outside the office and walked me to the breastfeeding support group I'd been attending biweekly. She assured me that I had other options and advised me to talk to the lactation consultant when I got there to find out what those options were. We walked together. Me, so very postpartum, tears streaming down my face, and Rose, hugely pregnant, determined to walk out her "overdue" baby at 42 weeks pregnant so that she wouldn't have to be induced the next day.[66]

I'll never forget Rose dropping me off at the yoga studio that hosted the group: her face frozen at the doorway, wanting so much to be on the other side with those of us who were lucky enough to have our babies safely outside our bodies; me, bleary-eyed with tears, barely able to muster a wave goodbye because I was so consumed with the fear and worry of the moment. Two women, on both sides of birth, both feeling quite miserable, both drowning in not-enoughness.

Once inside, I went straight to Andrea, my fave lactation consultant who I mentioned earlier and who ran this particular group. I told her the facts: "I am not enough."

---

[66] She woke up in labor the next morning! And I put "overdue" in quotes because we get quite fixated on estimated due dates (EDDs) in our culture, as if there's a deadline by which baby should be out, and anything after that is "late." In reality, babies can come on their own anywhere within a period of about 5 weeks around their EDD, and that's still "normal" and healthy. Heck, even a little earlier or later than that can be some variation of normal, too!

Those may not have been the exact words I spoke, but it's definitely what I was saying.

"The pediatrician says she hasn't gained enough weight."

"Put that baby on the scale," Andrea said assuredly.

At the doctor's office, baby girl had weighed in at 9 lbs 2 oz. Not enough. Andrea's scale read differently: 10 lbs 15 oz. I looked at her in shock as my heart skipped a beat.

"SHE WAS ENOUGH! I WAS ENOUGH! **I AM ENOUGH!**" It felt like victory.

Andrea continued, "Their scale is off. It happens all the time."

I felt so many things. Confusion. Rage. Relief. Indignation.

DO YOU SEE HOW THE EXPERT TOLD ME THAT I WAS NOT ENOUGH, WHEN IN FACT I WAS? AND I AM?

This happens to humans all over the world, young and old, on the daily. This traumatizing thing of being told that we are not enough.

Enough is enough.

It's time we decided to start believing something that feels better, and that actually is the truth: **we are enough.** It's time to start knowing that **we are enough** (because we are), stating it as fact (because it is), acting as if it's true (because it is), and surrounding ourselves with people and places and things and experiences that reflect that truth (because that's what we deserve).

This whole experience, which is something I can still manage to feel mad about half a decade later, was so powerful for me. It was the experience that taught me I needed to be more discerning. To begin trusting myself as the expert—if you'll recall, my first instinct at being told there was a problem with my girl's weight was total surprise and disbelief, because I felt that everything was great—and to surround myself with experts I trust as much as I trust myself. You know, like Andrea.[67]

Be Your Own Expert and Gather Your Team
Let me tell you what happened after that visit to the breastfeeding support group, where Andrea swooped in with an accurate scale to save the day: I called the pediatrician's office to shame them for their mistake and to prove to them that I was, indeed, **enough.**

You tell them! Said the voice in my head.

---

[67] I come from a family of medical professionals. I dreamed of being a doctor my entire childhood and into college. I have a tremendous amount of respect for the field of medicine, and for the individuals who care for others as my close family members do. When a doctor really hears and respects a patient, and makes recommendations to that end, it's a win for all. I've also experienced that sometimes, including in this case, medical providers offer misinformation rather than saying "I don't know" or referring patients to someone who does know. In this way, the power dynamic becomes problematic, planting the doctor safely in the ground of "I'm the Expert," and the patient in a space of "I believe everything you tell me." This concerns me deeply, and I wanted to tell you that in hopes it will help you make the shifts that I've made since this particular experience.

When they picked up the phone, I explained all that had happened, requesting that they re-weigh baby girl. The woman on the phone informed me that if I wanted to bring our baby back for another weight check, I'd need to pay for another visit. I was aghast. Angry, shocked, appalled, hurt. Again.

This was *their* mistake, I reiterated, sure she'd respond differently. I figured she'd soften, telling me to bring baby back by on my way home at no charge. Instead, she asked, "Would you like for us to put the lactation consultant's weight reading on your baby's medical record and delete the other one?" I couldn't believe it. I couldn't *believe* that having inaccurate data and offering medical advice based on that data—*advice that affects real lives*—seemed like a non-issue to them.

Rather than saying exactly what I was feeling, which is probably what I'd do if facing this same situation now (followed by writing a strongly worded letter to Dr. G. herself, sharing my experience with her directly), I gave up. I told her that we'd just come back for our next appointment and got off the phone.

We did go back to that practice eventually, but we switched pediatricians. We made an appointment with Dr. S., who had been the first pediatrician to see our baby in the hospital when she was born and whom we'd really liked, even though we'd already committed to be regular patients of Dr. G.

Anyway, we switched from Dr. G. to Dr. S., and at our next appointment, we told Dr. S. our story. I shared how *shamed* I'd felt by Dr. G.'s conviction that I was unable to provide enough milk for my baby and needed to supplement with formula. About how the office manager had handled our request for another weight check. Dr. S listened with full attention. At the conclusion, he looked into my eyes. "I'm so sorry she made you feel that way."

He told us that what happened was absolutely not okay with him, and shared that because of known issues weighing babies correctly, the office already had established a protocol of weighing the baby a second time if the first weight was lower than expected. In other words, this mistake never should have happened. When the medical assistant weighed my baby girl and her weight was lower than expected according to the growth curve noted on her records, the pediatrician herself should have re-weighed her. But she didn't. She took the assistant's recorded data at face value, decided not to double-check it, and gave medical advice that made me feel responsible for my baby's low weight gain. That made me feel not-enough. That treated *my baby*—a newborn!—as if she were not enough.

Dr. S. promised to discuss the incident with the entire practice at their next staff meeting. He promised to make it clear to them that this was absolutely unacceptable.

He made me feel like—you *know* now, don't you? —**the *most important person***. And he became our new pediatrician. Part of our team. A teammate I gathered with my newly found discernment.

What's the point of sharing all this with you? To demonstrate the importance of **gathering your team**, of course. Once you've committed to the Journey to Enoughness, it's important to surround yourself with people who can assist you on your journey by treating you as **the most important person** and encouraging you to treat your self like **the most important person**. I call these people your team.

They are your experts. They know things that you don't know, *and* they help you find the expert within yourself. They guide you to your own answers, because they know that YOU are your #1 expert; and they encourage you to trust yourself fully, because they know that is what it means to be enough. Your experts will know that nobody knows what's right for you, better than you—**YGTD**—and the best teammates will support you in remembering that too, especially when things get tough.

Having a team is not optional; it takes a village to live happily on this Earth and to fully serve one's purpose here. So, you need people. I need people. We *all* need people. People who are on our side. People who make us feel like **the most important person**. If you're feeling like maybe this doesn't apply to you, that you can do it *yourself*, I ask you: "How's that going for you?"

I suspect you'll find that shifting from going it alone to having the support of your (dream) team, will *also* mean shifting from struggle to knowing that, no matter what comes up, you and your team are exactly what you need.

Gathering your team of experts who will support you on the never-ending Journey to Enoughness is a bit of a chicken and the egg process. To gather a team we trust, we must trust ourselves and our instincts enough to determine who can support our growth, and to discern who isn't a good fit. And to really trust ourselves, most of us need people around us who encourage that self-trust and teach us to be our own experts. (Our team.)

When the doctors told me my first baby was too small in utero, I cried and worried. I was wracked with fear: of something being wrong with my baby and of it *being my fault*. I didn't trust myself. If my baby wasn't growing according to the Experts' measures, I felt sure that *I* was the problem. When, later, the pediatrician found her weight gain unimpressive and told me my baby needed formula because I couldn't produce enough milk, I had yet another mama meltdown, because, yet again, the problem was ME. I was not *enough*. I didn't trust myself. In both cases, I was already living in Not Enough when my experts-at-the-time (shall we call them ex-experts? Ex²perts?) reaffirmed my belief that I was not enough. I didn't trust myself, so I trusted them instead, despite how terrible it made me feel.

Had I trusted myself, I would have moved through both of these experiences differently. During pregnancy, I would have requested a different doctor to read my ultrasounds or to help me understand what was happening. I would have asked my OB for support in doing this, so that my hospital visits became informative and helpful, rather than a reason to go farther down my rabbit hole. If that didn't help, I would have found another place to give birth where I felt more heard and more supported. In the second instance, I would have spoken my truth to Dr. G. in the moment about how not-enough she was making me feel. I would have then switched doctors and made sure someone at that practice told everybody else that the way I'd been treated was absolutely unacceptable. (Oh wait, I did do that one! Go me!)

I've since realized that, just like it's not our fault when we're living in Not Enough or when we're judging ourselves, it's not our fault when we don't trust ourselves either. None of us are at fault when we trust "experts" more than we trust our own instincts, even if we think we should "know better" by now. For most of us, lack of self-trust is a result of lifelong conditioning, and if we're going to change that, we must make an effort.

At the time of these experiences, I "knew" that I was not enough, and *anyone* who confirmed it was just speaking the Truth. Especially if they were an "expert." They were making my not-enoughness even more true.

Except it wasn't true. It isn't true. And it's never been true.

I am *always* enough.

And it's only because of my team—the people I've surrounded myself with who remind me regularly that ***I am the most important person***—that I've learned to trust that.

Like I said, this is a chicken and the egg thing. As I've trusted myself more, I've gathered more and more experts onto my team. I now have *so many* trusted experts in my life, because I trust myself to choose teammates who support me in being my very-enough self. I *always* have someone to go to. So many people I trust!

Regardless of what kind of team you're putting together (school, work, surprise party planning, a new business venture, health, finding a home, childcare, healing from trauma, travel, and all the other things we could use a team for, which is basically all the things), it's important to know whom to ask about what. Sometimes, a member of your team may have expertise that helps you, but they don't have the specific insight you're needing in a particular situation. Not every expert is expert at everything.

When my first daughter was 18 months old, I had foot surgery. The anesthesiologist on duty told me that because of the anesthesia I'd have to pump and dump. I asked if he was sure; I didn't want to waste all that milk! He said he really didn't know for sure and "better safe than sorry."

I had taken great pains in choosing this particular medical team, selecting them as my experts, and yet, when something came up that didn't feel good, I trusted my instinct to push for more information. Knowing that many doctors lack lactation training—and because I'd already lived through the trauma of another medical professional telling me I couldn't safely feed my child with my body—I knew better than to take this guy's word for it when it came to breast milk (though I absolutely would when it came to anesthesia!). He was not the expert I needed, and because I'd surrounded myself with experts who had helped me trust myself, I took matters into my own hands. How? I texted Andrea, my other expert. She texted back that it was safe to nurse my baby, and she explained why. I shared my findings with the anesthesiologist, and he shrugged, saying, "Yeah, she probably knows *way* better than I do."

When we gather our team, what we're really doing is surrounding ourselves with people who will give us the kind of support we truly need. People who will give us what we are really hoping for each time we ask for help: a way to come home to ourselves; to our own knowing. We're deciding who is on our short list of people to call when something big comes up, who to share our successes with, and who to trust at their word, both because of their *actual* knowledge and expertise *and* because they make us feel like **the most important person.** Now that you know that your team MUST be comprised of people who you deeply trust **and** *that you must also trust yourself*...know also:

The thing about your team is: **YGTD.**

As I've said, that pediatrician who misdiagnosed me with low milk supply based on incorrect weighing did not stay on my team. Andrea, on the other hand, who helped me through that harrowing experience and who was on the other end of the text when I needed expert lactation backup? She'll be on my team as long as I'm lactating and supporting those who are. What's the difference between these two experts? One used the data in front of her to *prove* that I was not enough (despite office protocol that directed her otherwise), and the other tuned in to my emotions on the spot, supporting me in identifying a plan of action that actually took me and my experience into consideration. Of these two experts, one served me well. The other most certainly did not.

Who are the people you *trust*? The ones who treat you as though **you are the most important person**? Who help you be you?

Keep them.

Who are the people who make you feel not-enough? The ones who fill your head with doubt? Who make you feel judged and shamed?

Give them the pink slip.

Not everyone gets to *be* on your team and, not everyone gets to *stay* on your team. This is true for ALL relationships in your life. Whether it's an internet friend, a medical provider, a partner, or an accountant, if there is anyone currently on your team who is not fully supporting you, it's time for them to go. You're the captain of your team, and **you get to decide** who's on it. And off! Only the people who know their stuff, who care about you, who make you feel heard—only those people get to stay. And they all have one thing in common: they treat you like **the most important person**. Not only that, they remind you to *treat yourself* like **the most important person**. Because they *know* that when **you** are *truly taken care of, everyone around you benefits.*

It's important to note that teams change. As the team captain, you get to decide whom to ask, and for what, and as you experience how your team responds in moments of need, you get to decide who goes and who stays. In all of this gathering and shifting and re-convening of your team, trust yourself.

Is the idea of cutting someone from the team making you queasy? You're not alone. (**You're never alone!**) Deciding who goes and then communicating that decision isn't always easy. If you're anything like me, you stick with people—partners, [68] medical providers, hairstylists, baristas, dry cleaners, babysitters, fill in the blank here—as long as you can, and often way longer than you should.

Why do we do this? If you're like me, it's because you are *loyal*. You don't give up on people. In the past, you've always gained a sense of control or power from sticking with what and whom you know. And for many people, sticking things out is also a source of self-worth, which we can be reluctant to give up if we're struggling with our own enoughness. So, if you haven't created the time and space to truly ask yourself if there's anyone you need to release from your team, that's okay. There's no time like the present.

Take a moment to think about your team and consider each teammate. Ask yourself:

What do I need right now? Can this person provide it? If not, is there someone else on my team who can? Is there anyone on my team who is making me feel not-enough? Is this person the right fit for who I am now?

---

[68] I'm not talking about you, dear husband—just the ones who came before you!

It can be challenging at first to create the space we need to ask questions like these, because sometimes, the answers can indicate that we need to let go of people in our life that we've been holding onto. The answers can be big. And scary. Often, they require us to get *reallllly* vulnerable, with ourselves and others. They require us to surrender to our truth and to let go of what's not serving us in order to create space for what we truly want. This can bring up a lot of fear:

If I get clear about what I really need and want, who will I be then? Will I still need this person? What if I don't need them anymore? How can I live without them / disappoint them / let them go? Now that I know this is true, do I have to act on it?

This last one is a doozy. For those of us who are committed to the journey, once we discover our truth about what will support us, it's impossible to ignore it for long. And if we do choose to ignore it—to keep people on our team and in our lives who make us feel not-enough—something usually happens to force a change. All that said, the biggest truth here is that when it comes to your team, **you get to decide.** You don't have to cut a teammate until you're ready. But being aware that something needs shifting, can remind you of your *true* (and infinite!) power.

If you're reading this and you're feeling some self-doubt, I invite you to *create the space* that you need to ask these tough questions; to really open up; to go inside your most important self to the place where *the answers already are.* While some people can do this anytime, anywhere, I've found that for most people, discerning *what and whom* you need and want is a *deeply* challenging process, and it requires dedicated time and space to explore.

That doesn't mean you can't do it. You CAN. And, you can LISTEN TO THE ANSWERS. You already know what you need and what you want, and if you find yourself thinking, "No I don't," remember: **you are your own expert.**

You are the one who knows YOU best. You are the one who gets to decide, about EVERYTHING in your life. You are the one who, on the Journey to Enoughness, truly trusts yourself. Truly listens. Truly Hears YOU. You are the one who tells the truth. The one who cries with you and holds your own hand. You are the one who laughs with you and who delights in your joy. You are the one who never, ever leaves you. Who treats you as **the most important person**, always, and in all ways.

If you *choose* to be.

Being your own expert doesn't mean that everything will be perfect and go smoothly. *Every* journey has bumps, unexpected twists and turns, steep inclines that challenge you, and downhill segments that simultaneously exhilarate you and scare the shit out of you. The Journey to Enoughness is no exception. However, choosing to **be your own expert** *does* mean that you can, and will, trust yourself and your team, which means that **you are never alone.** And even if you feel like you are, **you are always enough.**

Ask for Help. Receive It. Be Glad You Did.
Ahhhh, *asking* for help. It's challenging sometimes, no?

And yet, asking for help can also be such an amazing experience. When we trust ourselves enough to ask for *exactly* what we need, and when we trust others well enough to be vulnerable and clear with them—to be vulnerabrave, really—we always receive *exactly* what we need. Sometimes, getting what we need looks like getting what we want. Other times, getting what we need looks nothing like getting what we thought we wanted, and usually, this leads us to new opportunities for growth. Either way, the act of asking for help supports us in being more our*selves.* It also improves how we serve others, because when we are in touch with our own needs, we're also better able to intuit others' needs. Talk about a win!

Asking for help, and the emotional journey that it takes for us to get comfortable doing that, is another topic I could write a whole book about. Most of us have a lot to move through in order to ask for what we really need. You see, in asking for help, we must identify what we *really* want, which means sorting through our insecurities about what we do and don't deserve. And as we already talked about, most of us have to create the space and time in our lives to do that. And then, once we've identified what we want/need, we have to share information with the people in our lives who can provide the support that we need, regardless of how we think they might respond to this new version of our selves—the one who knows we are enough.

Trusting yourself enough to get clear on what you really want and then ask for the help you truly need is a huge step on the Journey to Enoughness, and like most of the things we've been talking about, with practice, it can become second nature.

This year, in the month leading up to my daughter's fifth birthday, I was busy: I attended births three out of four weekends and participated in an advanced doula training on the fourth, all while churning out this book. On top of that, I was on call, meaning I could be called away for a birth at any moment and for any length of time. Leo and I kept trying to choose a date for a birthday party, but each time we looked at the calendar, I realized I might not be able to make it. We decided to wait; to celebrate after things died down.

After my final client gave birth, I invited a few of my big girl's closest friends and their parents to a casual birthday playdate in our apartment—think kids running around shrieking happily while parents enjoyed an in-home happy hour. Throw in some temporary tattoos, a few packs of stick-on earrings, pizza, and cupcakes, and you've got a party. About midway through, I was in the kitchen frosting the cupcakes when one child came in asking for juice and another appeared requesting help with a tattoo.

In the past, my first reaction would have been, "Give me a minute, I'll be right there" followed by an eye roll or a heavy sigh. The old I'm-the-one-fully-responsible-for-everything-happening-here default would have kicked in, and I would have felt resentful and alone.

Thankfully, I remembered: *I am never alone*.

In fact, a father had asked awhile back if he could do anything to help, and in that moment, I'd said no. But right when these two children asked for help, he reappeared, and I realized that just because I'd turned down his earlier offer didn't mean that I couldn't ask for what I needed now.

"Eric, can you help her get a juice?" I know this seems like a small request, and yet, IT FELT LIKE SUCH A BIG DEAL!

Anyway, Eric got the juice, and I finished up the cupcakes, while another parent swooped in to help the second child with her tattoo.[69] Rather than insisting that all the other

---

[69] Isn't it amazing how, as soon as you ask for help, *more help comes, including* help you didn't ask for at all? It's like someone out/up there knows what we need. As if *we are connected in ways we cannot see*. AMAZING. And, when you

adults enjoy themselves while inwardly feeling resentful about having to take care of everything, I allowed myself to be supported. Then, I thanked them and continued to focus on the cupcakes. A few minutes later, I was sitting on my couch, drinking a beer, and laughing with friends, all while the kids continued to play.

I got to have *fun.*

Wooooooooooot!

Because I asked for help.

The old me *never* asked for help. Never. And if someone offered, she responded with a cheerful-sounding (yet actually quite cheerless), "No, thank you!" For most of my life, I routinely rejected help without even pausing to consider whether or not *it might actually be helpful to me*!

We do this, don't we? We stop ourselves from asking for help, believing we shouldn't need it. We decline help that's offered, thinking that accepting it is a sign of weakness. When someone does help, it's challenging for us to receive it. We judge ourselves and miss out on opportunities for connection, when we'd do better to say "thank you" and feel the gratitude for the support that's available to us. Accepting help has a positive ripple effect for ourselves *and* those who choose to help us. So why don't we do it?

I've got good news: this tendency to reject help is not our fault. Just like our learned not-enoughness, the judgment that comes with it, and our propensity to distrust ourselves, all

---

open up to asking for and receiving help, this phenomenon soon becomes not surprising in the least.

this crazy-making behavior has been modeled for us, in one relationship or another.

Like many of you, I grew up with a mother who did All The Things for our family. At our house, she was the project manager *and* she ran all the projects. She had help from us, sure, and she recognized the value of investing money in helpers, such as housekeepers and babysitters (which she thankfully had the means to do), but when something needed to get done, it was my mom who did it. It's no wonder my first sentence was "I can do it myself."

The good news is, even if this kind of behavior is deeply ingrained, we have the power to change it. We make this shift by accepting help when it's offered, and by reaching out, actively, to ask for the support we need.

A few years after my first pump-free trip to that yoga retreat, I headed back to Ojai for the annual weekend away for my friend Emily and me. I knew well ahead of time that with my second sweet babe staying with her grandparents while I was yog-ing, I'd need to figure out the milk sitch, and this time, things were going to be *different*: I wasn't going to be consumed by scarcity. In fact, I decided I wasn't going to spend *any* time or energy expressing extra milk for the trip at all. Instead, I decided to get all vulnerabrave and ask for help.

So I did.

I posted in my favorite Facebook mom group:

> "I'm coming to CA for the following weekend in October. Does anyone have any extra milk in your freezer stash that you could spare for my baby while she's with her grandparents and I'm away yog-ing?"

When I posted, I felt anxious. I wondered if I'd be judged, if others would think I'm weird. If that would make me feel not enough. But at the same time, I knew better already. It was like a super quick visit to Not Enough. And then I waited to receive the help I'd asked for.

The responses I received were immediate and so, so kind. Months ahead of the trip, I had (A) a list of three moms who would have more than enough breastmilk ready for my husband to pick up when we got into town and I headed to the mountains, and (B) a grand total of zero units of worry about what my baby would consume while I was high on a mountain, and high on life.

I asked for the support I desired, and in doing so, I opened myself up to receiving it.

My friends, you can do this too. You can *choose* to do this.

I'm talking about milk sharing,[70] sure, but I'm also talking about *everything in life.*

---

[70] I'm a huge, huge fan of milk sharing—giving your breastmilk to someone else for their baby, or accepting someone else's milk for yours. Not sure if it's safe? Feeling weird about asking others for milk, when somebody might need it more than you do? Or because it's weird and taboo to share breastmilk? Talk to your team, as I did. And consider that, just like with hand expression, when it comes to feeding your baby, you may have more options than you think. Another person's milk might be one of those options, and your life might be easier if you choose to ask for and receive that support. Milk sharing is such an easy way to help someone else, or be helped, *massively*. With rare exceptions, it's safe to share breastmilk with others. And it helps us remember: **you are never alone, there's more where that**

Wherever you are, whatever you need, you can:
1. Ask yourself what you need.
2. Ask others to help you, however it is you desire to be helped, without fear.
3. Surround yourself with the people and things and places that make you feel safe enough to ask for the support you need.
4. *Be* the support that others need.

This last point is not because karma (although yeah, karma!), but because we *all* deserve to be supported, and we all deserve to support others. In fact, the experience of wholeheartedly supporting others is something that *each of us needs* to fully integrate our own Journey to Enoughness.

It's a cycle. Of giving and receiving. Of asking for help and offering it to others. Once we've learned how to ask for exactly what we need and how to receive that help gratefully and graciously, we can move on to setting ourselves up to get that help consistently: in the moments we need it, and in the long-term. We keep gathering our team, releasing the relationships that aren't serving us, and becoming teammates to the people around us. We are our own experts. And we expertly serve others who are on their own Journey. We repeat. And repeat. And repeat.

We do all this because we know we all deserve it. **We know we are enough**.

In the past, I didn't ask for help because I felt like I didn't deserve it. Now, I know that I do. Because even when I need

---

came from, **we are enough**, and **each of us is the most important person**—a.k.a. we all deserve support. See the Resources section for some of my favorite ways to engage in and support milk sharing.

help, **I am** *always* **enough**. If you find asking for and receiving help challenging, maybe you're like me: you feel *you don't deserve it*. You're clinging to the notion that you're *supposed* to "do it all." You don't want to disappoint *anyone*. You thrive on being in charge, but you feel overwhelmed by it too—even *alone* at times.

My friends, **you are never alone.** WE are never alone.

When I say "we," I'm talking about you and me and everyone else who is on a Journey to Enoughness. *We* will be the ones who help when others need it, if given the chance to do so. Which means we need to get comfortable with asking for the help we need and receiving it, both gratefully and gracefully.

When we learn how to ask for and receive the help we need, we teach those who help us how to ask for the support that they need, too. Asking for help and learning to receive it is hands down one of the most powerful ways to lead by example in your life, transforming the lives of those around you.

Take a moment right now to make a list of 10 things you need help with. This isn't challenging, right? You can probably think of more like 100. If so, list away. If not, that's okay too.

If you catch yourself thinking, *No one can do that but me / I just have to figure it out / I'm the only one who knows how to do that*, know that **you are not alone (not ever!)**, and you have to ask for help in order to receive it. Be gentle with yourself. Remember, resisting help is something that's been modeled for us and we've had a lot of practice doing it!

Take a moment to close your eyes, take a deep breath, and just *be* for a moment. Get quiet. (No small task right? But just do it. You *can*. Right now.) Now, tell yourself, "**You are enough**. You can have anything you want. You deserve support from others in order to live your best life."

Then ask again: *What do I need help with at this moment?*

Make your list. 10 things. Go ahead—you've got this.

Now look at your list. Find the task that you would like support with, first. This might be a task that you know you can pass on to someone else; a task that's making you feel very not-enough right now; or a time-sensitive task, so you'd like support with it sooner rather than later. What kind of support do you need? Who can you ask for help? Is there someone on your team who has the expertise you need? Or do you need to seek out someone new?

If you start feeling overwhelmed, take a breath. Imagine what it would feel like to get that help. It's already better, isn't it? A weight lifted off your chest, a feeling of lightness and human connection?

So do it. Ask for help. Receive help. Practice both of these. It'll be good for you. And you'll be glad you did.

Healing into Enoughness

Sometimes, before we can begin asking for the help we need, we have some healing to do. We may be caught up in some not-enough story that's really holding us hostage. This has definitely been true for me, which is part of why I'm a huge, huge fan of healing. So huge in fact that I'm saving a lot of what I've got to say about it for my next book. (Really! You can quote me on that.)

FRANCIE WEBB

I do want to share one particularly powerful story of healing in my life, because it's been so key on my Journey to Enoughness. It's a long one, and I've purposely kept it short here (because, again, another book), but I trust that what I choose to tell you here and now is going to serve you *perfectly.* It's going to be enough for you. For now.

I'd like to tell you a true story about a little girl named Catherine.

She was born in 1995 in Lynchburg, Virginia, and one night, when she was only 11 weeks old, I was entrusted as her babysitter. I watched her (and her big brother, aged 2), while her parents went to a wedding. I'd never babysat for them before, and they'd never left Catherine with anyone. I think they felt comfortable hiring me because they found me through a friend.

I was 14 then and had cared for many children, both as a babysitter and as an older sibling of young twins. For someone my age, I had a lot of experience. I was a competent and confident babysitter.

After a pretty normal (read: stressful) night caring for an infant and a toddler, I was getting some juice for the toddler, who was supposed to be in bed by then but who just wouldn't settle down. My plan was to give him his juice, then walk back upstairs to check on Catherine, whom I'd put down to sleep about an hour earlier. Before I could head up, the door opened, and her parents walked in. Her mom took over with big brother, and her dad took me home.

Shortly after he dropped me off, the phone rang. It wasn't uncommon for my father, a physician, to get phone calls late at night when he was on call. But this was no ordinary call.

Catherine was dead.

At some point after I put her down to sleep, she stopped breathing. By the time her mom checked on her, after I'd left, it was too late.

Catherine—a name I couldn't say out loud for years after the fact—had died in her crib.

I was 14

and

I was 100% sure it was *my* fault.

Despite the fact that everyone, including Catherine's parents, assured me that her death was not my fault, I knew the Truth, and I dealt with that Truth day in and day out. I moved through the world always feeling that I was somehow at fault for all the bad things that happened in my life and even in the lives of others, in some cases. Though I wasn't consciously aware of the power this huge burden of guilt held over me, it was ever-present. With me always, and in all ways.

I carried that feeling for YEARS.

It wasn't that others weren't supportive—they were. Friends, family and future romantic partners were all quite loving when I shared the story—an experience I always used as a barometer to see if they could *really* love me, knowing what I'd "done." But I kept feeling surprised by their reaction—*of course it wasn't your fault!*—regardless of how many times I heard it said. I felt as if I was the only one who knew the truth. And that made it even harder to carry. *No one else* understood. Catherine was my deep dark secret. The skeleton in my closet. The proof that *I was **not** enough*.

I refused every offer of help when it came to more formal support, like therapy and grief counseling; I didn't feel I deserved it. What's more, I thought if I got help, I'd have to

115

really *deal with it*, which felt terrifying beyond belief. Impossible.

I finally **did** get help in the form of therapy, thankfully. By then, it was seven years later, and I was so scared of dealing with her death that in the weeks approaching my first therapy appointment, I had a full-blown anxiety attack in the middle of a retail store at Christmastime. The store was teeming with people in the usual holiday shopping rush, and I needed only one item—holiday cards to send to friends. As I approached the register, I couldn't find my wallet, and suddenly, everything around me started spinning; I felt as if I couldn't breathe or even feel my own body. My boyfriend at the time (who, to be clear, is *not* my husband) was standing next to me, and though I can't remember what he said while it was happening, I will never forget that he later told me I'd "gone crazy." When I came to, I ran to the car. My wallet was on the seat. This experience made me *extra* afraid to go to therapy, and it also helped me understand that therapy was exactly what I needed. And so, I went—*thank you, God*—and I soon began healing.

I'm telling you right now: healing from trauma, any kind of trauma, is no small thing. It's really fucking scary, and in moments, the burden of healing can feel far too heavy to carry. And sometimes, even after you've consciously set the intention to heal, you wish you'd never started the healing process in the first place, because it doesn't always *feel* so "healing." In fact, sometimes the process of healing can feel downright awful. Like you're going backwards instead of forwards. Reliving hurt that you never wanted to feel again, and doing it by *choice*. The truth is: sometimes, in order to truly heal, we have to allow ourselves to fully experience things we don't want to feel, because the only way out is through. Healing is part of the ever-challenging, always-awesome Journey to Enoughness.

Healing through the trauma of Catherine's death was crucial for me. It's one of the main reasons that I was eventually able to trust myself enough to be able to birth and feed my babies and that, when I encountered challenges feeding my first baby, I trusted myself enough to try hand expression. Because I knew that if I could heal from this—from the trauma of feeling responsible for the death of an infant—I could do anything, *including* getting milk out with my hands. Through my healing, I was empowered.

The truth is: **each of us has power, and it's in our hands**. To decide how we respond to the unexpected things that happen in our lives—really, to *all* the things that happen in our lives—and to make meaning of them as we choose. And even if we've been living with old wounds, believing all the terrible things we've made them mean about us, we can always choose differently, if we choose to heal.

Now that I've had time and space and so much healing, now that I've received more love than I ever believed I deserved (and now I know that I deserve it *all*), I get to consciously choose the meaning of Catherine's death, and of her *life*. I get to decide how to hold that experience. What to make it mean. And the decision to hold her life and death as an integral part of my life's journey rather than as a skeleton in my closet completely changes the way I move through the world. I know that I'm enough, now, because I have HEALED, and because I am *still* healing.

This journey of healing takes time, patience, and true vulnerabravery. Some healing processes may feel "done" or "over," and we can let old wounds go. Some may feel as if you have to start anew each day, and that's okay too. Once you recognize and accept that healing is always a journey, you'll find that fear falls away, and that will help you get even better at healing, now and forever.

117

You may be asking, "How do I begin?" The path is different for everyone, and there is no Right place to start. You can start anywhere.

Start here.

Ask yourself:

What do I need to heal? What do I need to let go of so that I can feel ENOUGH?

I'm not claiming to be The Expert in your life, but here's what I do know: If you heal what needs healing, you'll feel better. Yes, healing takes deep, meaningful, for-better-or-worse commitment. It's challenging, messy, annoying, and at times, excruciatingly painful. And yet, it's always worth it.

Always.

You Can Do the Impossible Thing
As we move through life, some things can feel downright impossible. Really big things, like healing. Yet we do them. And after we do them, things change.

When my second daughter was born, I did a really big thing: I birthed her by myself. This was not something I planned on doing, and in fact, it was something I never thought I could or would do. And doing this big, impossible thing changed the course of my life. (As big, impossible things do!)

After the birth of our first child, Leo and I decided that if and when we had another, we wanted to change the setting, creating a different experience than the first time around. The goal was less anxiety, more support. So when I got pregnant for the second time, we began planning a home birth and meticulously **gathering our team** of experts: a fantastic and highly-experienced midwife, Kristen; her assistant, Chloe; our favorite doula, Karla; a photographer, Michelle; a babysitter, Krista, to pick up our big girl; two dear friends, Rose (remember Rose? 42 weeks pregnant and supporting me as I cried?) and Marisa, who would come to provide emotional and physical support; and my mom, who hoped to attend either in person or on FaceTime, depending on how quickly things progressed. Everything was in place. We were open to things unfolding as they were meant to, but we also had a plan and a team to support us in having things go the way we wanted them to, and we knew that they would be there for us on The Big Day.

Then the day came. Once my labor began, things progressed far more quickly than anyone could have imagined. In fact, my entire labor was only about an hour long. And, from the moment it started, it was *intense.*

It was still dark when the contractions began, just before 5 in the morning. I called Kristen and Karla—both said they would be on the way shortly. I woke Leo up by handing him the phone and saying, "Karla wants to talk to you." (I figured her voice would be a lot calmer than mine, and I wanted to ease him into the surprising news that today, a week before our due date, was going to be our baby's birthday.) I called my two friends, who didn't answer, and then the photographer. I didn't call the babysitter, because our older daughter was fast asleep in her bedroom; I prayed she'd stay that way. Within 25 minutes, most of our team was en route, and Leo busied himself with setting up the birth tub while I moved around, trying to get comfortable. We both thought we'd have everything ready by the time our team arrived.

There was a wrench in our plan: to get water from the shower to the birth tub, we needed to attach a hose, and we were missing an actual wrench to do the job. We'd intended to go to the hardware store later that day, but you know, the best-laid plans and #birth and all that. As Leo tried to MacGyver the situation, I tried to keep my cool. And I did a pretty good job of it. In fact, when I talked to the photographer, I'd assured her that she could take the subway instead of a cab. She didn't need to rush. We had *plenty* of time. "At least an hour," I'd said. So calm.

Less than twenty minutes later, I found myself

alone

on my bed

with a tiny human barreling her way out of my body.

I was racked with shock.

Like What. The Fuck. Is THIS?!

Painful, intense beyond belief. This child was ACTUALLY barreling her way out of my body. There was only one way out. And it was HAPPENING. NOOOOOOOW. Fucking **NOW**. And my team wasn't here yet.

My conscious mind didn't want the baby to come yet—I *wanted* to wait for my team to arrive so I could be supported through this the way I'd planned—but I also didn't *feel* alone. Not in the least. I may have been alone on my bed, but the truth is that I was not alone. Not at *all*. And, deep down, I knew it. I felt that truth in my core, and it strengthened me.

Even though my team wasn't all physically present, the way I thought I needed them to be—with their hands on me, massaging my shoulders and offering me water in my special straw cup, pressing on my hips and telling me I could do it, holding my hands and brushing my hair out of my face, just BEing with me—they were still there.

All the work we'd done in preparation for this, our second birth; all of the healing we'd done from the anxiety of preparing for our first child; it all paid off that day. It had prepared me to **do the impossible thing**.[71] All of those experiences, and the people who facilitated them, were inside my body and surrounding me, as I moved through this second labor.

I was alone.

And

I had my whole team with me.

---

[71] The hour-long visits with my midwife on my couch just getting to know me and treating me like **the most important person**; the moments when she showed my big girl how to listen to baby's heartbeat in my belly, telling her, "Your baby is so strong!"; the dinner with our doula to talk about the birth (which we'd done even though I'd felt *sure* I didn't need an appointment, since, you know, I'd done this before); the conference call Karla organized with my mom and two friends, and my mom tearing up and thanking everyone for caring for me, *her* baby; the advice from my midwife to move through my nervousness about asking my mom to be present at my birth, which made me feel extra vulnerable; the actual asking, when my mom told me she would love to be there, and we made plans for her to come when she could or be on FaceTime if things progressed too quickly; the decisions to avoid testing and ultrasounds that we'd had so many of last time, all made with the expertise and advice of our team in hand.

FRANCIE WEBB

Moments before I'd walked into my room and gotten on the bed, I'd made the conscious decision to *surrender*.

Surrender, I said to myself. *Just go inside.*

And so I did. Off to the bedroom. On to the bed. To go inside. To do this VERY BIG thing. This *biggest* thing.

As I lay on my bed focused on my commitment to surrender, I did the next thing to came to mind: I called my mom. She waited on the phone while I had a tough contraction. After I was through it, I told her I'd call her again later, either when I needed her or after the whole thing was over. A few minutes after getting off the phone with her, I was still on the bed in what **definitely** felt like (and actually turned out to be) the late stages of labor, when Leo came in to tell me the bad news: the birth tub just wasn't going to happen. Even though I'd told him that his *only* job was to get the tub ready for me—my desire to give birth in the water was second only to my desire for a home birth—I couldn't have cared less in that moment.

"DON'T TALK TO ME ABOUT THE TUB!!!"

In that very moment, my water broke. The dramatic way, like you see in movies:

POP!

Massive *gush*.

I got on my hands and knees. "Call the midwife and tell her my water broke!" I yelled at Leo. He picked up the phone. Because I was a human in labor, my next thought was, "WHY IS HE ON THE PHONE RIGHT NOW?!?!?" I was so annoyed. But I was also too busy to stay there.

I kept laboring.

I kept breathing.

Leo returned to the room. I told him to clean up the bed behind me, because I'd started pooping. (Yeah, I said it. Shit happens during birth, my friends. It really does. I'm not ashamed to tell you this truth, if you don't already know it. Most humans poop at one point or another during the birth process, and most of us are too embarrassed to ever talk about it. There is a lot of shame around birth, and around others seeing our bodies (our *selves*) in this astonishing act that we are meant to do, however we do it. This process often involves poop. The shame stops here. These are natural bodily functions we're talking about!) I didn't want the poop in my birth photo. There was this photo I'd been dreaming of, one that captured an image of my sweet baby in the moment he or she first came out of my body and into the world.

Leo sprayed the bed (and my feet and calves) with cleaning spray, covered my shit with paper towels, and picked it up, gagging the whole time. In my labor brain, I thought, "WHY IS HE SPRAYING ME?! WHY IS HE GAGGING?!"[72] As shit got

---

[72] Another thing not everyone talks about is how, during labor, a person giving birth experiences a massive shift in brain activity. We shift from our rational brain, known as the neocortex, into our middle brain, also known as our mammalian brain. This means that when our birth processes are otherwise undisturbed by outside forces, we literally go to a primal space. So things outside of us, and the words that come out of our mouths about them, may not make sense. We're focused on doing the thing, rather than trying to do many of the things we do in our daily lives, like stringing words into cohesive sentences or listening to others. Our primary, and perhaps only, function becomes going inside

handled, my thoughts shifted to the next most pressing matter. [73]

"I NEED TO KNOW WHERE THE BABY IS," I thought.

I reached inside and felt it.

You know what "it" is, don't you?

The baby's head. She was *right...**there**.*

"CALL THE DOULA AND TELL HER I CAN FEEL THE BABY'S HEAD!"

Picture: Leo, back in the hallway on the phone, and me, still on the bed, breathing through the final contractions, feeling for the umbilical cord, noticing a smushy spot at the top of baby's head, and hoping against hope it isn't the cord, because I know that indicates a cord prolapse, which is when the cord drops into the cervix below the baby's head, and pushing poses a risk for the baby. Again, "WHY IS HE ON THE PHONE?!?!?"

I stayed on hands and knees—the same position I'd birthed our first child in—confident it would help prevent this baby from getting stuck. She was coming, and I had to help her. I had to receive her.

And oh—I needed a picture!

"GET! CAMERA!" I yelled.

---

ourselves to help the humans we've created, come out of our bodies.
[73] Ha! This was a pressing matter indeed. There was definitely *press*ure—the most intense of my life.

In that moment, the moment right after I yelled for Leo to get the camera and right before my baby came barreling/sliding/gliding[74] into my arms, the possibility of fear flitted through my body. Like a whisper.

I heard it.

I felt it.

I acknowledged it.

I decided to pray.

To pray in stead of fear.

To the baby. To God. To every being who's ever lived. I prayed.

"I need you to be okay. *AND* I need you to let me *know* that you're okay."

---

[74] Someone later described my birth, in a comment on Facebook to someone else, as follows: "It sounds like the baby just slipped on out!" My immediate reaction was: *THERE WAS NO SLIPPING ON OUT.* I felt that her words minimized my experience, since I had surrendered so *actively* to get to these final moments of her birth, *and* because I had taken steps to determine what I needed to do to help her come out at the end. Also: it was so intensely painful. Her words suggested that our birth had been easy, and it wasn't—a fast birth doesn't mean an easy one. All of that said: My actions, and hers, culminated in her coming right on out. So I guess you could call this whole thing a team effort.

FRANCIE WEBB

In the most calm, present, and tactical moment of my life, I envisioned my sweet baby coming out of me and looking, as they say, "perfect." Then I pictured her crying a healthy cry. In that moment, I felt a flood of relief in my body.

I surrendered fully.

I fluttered my lips.[75]

Hard. Twice.

I reached back to guide her head out as gently as I could.

She spun as she entered the world, turning her body so that she was facing me as she moved from the back of my body to the front. I received her into my hands, my eyes fixed fiercely on her face, my lips still moving in their final flutter. I looked at her, and she looked okay. She looked beautiful. I listened, and she cried a healthy, "I'M HERE!" cry. She let me know she was okay.

It happened exactly as I had just envisioned, moments earlier.

I looked at the clock, knowing that *somebody* would need to know what time she was born. I memorized the numbers. Looking back at my baby, I greeted her, smiling. "Hiiiiiiiiii!" Then I turned to my husband, who, *in a shocking twist*, walked out of the room!

"WHERE ARE YOU GOING?!" I yelled.

---

[75] "Horse lips," they/we call it in birth work. It opens the sphincters. Look it up!

"The photographer's here," he replied. "I'm going to let her in!"

What happened next was precisely how I'd dreamed it: I rested in the comfort of my own bed, caring for my baby, as I received all the support I hoped for from my team. True, it didn't happen quite as we'd planned; I had imagined they'd all arrive *before* the birth and be there to support me *through* the whole process. And yet, the way it happened was exactly what I needed, because it allowed me to do the most impossible thing I'd ever done in my life, *all by myself*. And in the hours, days and weeks after, they were all there for me, holding me with so much love and care through the part that really mattered—the process of healing.

They gathered in our home—one or two at a time, gently and quietly—in the hour or so after my babe was born. The photographer, Michelle, was first on the scene, not even a full minute after the actual birth happened. She walked in, ready to photograph her very first birth, and I, holding a minute-old baby, crouched on the bed, suddenly had zero clue what to do with said baby. I looked right at Michelle, and I *think* I said, "WHAT THE FUCK JUST HAPPENED?!"

She *may* have said those same words right back to me. Then she started taking pictures. As she began photographing this sweet and shocking day, Leo and I called the midwife, asking what to do next. I followed her directions, lying down with the baby and putting a towel over her. Next Leo called my mom, whom I'd spoken to no more than 15 minutes earlier, to let her know that baby was here and that we were both safe and healthy.

Soon, Karla arrived. She helped baby girl and me get comfortable and perched herself next to us, assuring me that baby would indeed find the breast on her own. She put a straw to my lips, as my daughter nursed for the first time, reminding me of my own body's needs. Later that day, she also reminded me that I'd recently confided my biggest fear: that the baby would come before anyone on the birth team arrived. That I would be *alone*.

"It's almost like you manifested it!" she said. I didn't have any recollection of that, at the time, and yet—wow! It made some kind of cosmic sense, hearing it after the fact.

Kristen, our midwife, arrived next—hugging me and telling me how proud she was, saying she *knew* I could do it. We FaceTimed my friends who were supposed to come, and their jaws dropped when I showed them the baby at my breast. We laughed and cried and exclaimed at the wonder of it all. Soon, Kristen's assistant Chloe arrived, and everyone began taking care of all the things: the placenta; the cutting of the cord; my first trip to the bathroom; cleaning up and changing the sheets; washing a fresh load of cloth diapers, to soften them; our big girl waking up and meeting baby; reading a book about being a big sister; breakfast in bed for our new family of four.

I'm so grateful for my team, for everything they did both before and after I gave birth to support me, and for the fact that I trusted myself enough to honor what I really wanted for this second birth, enough to gather the team I needed to support me in making that happen. And I didn't stop there. Healing from this birth took longer than expected and felt far more challenging than healing from my first birth, and there were so many opportunities for me to slip back into my old default patterns of feeling not-enough.[76] I kept relying on my

---

[76] After all, I now had two children to attend to, and a pelvic floor that needed extra care after birthing said babies. I also suffered from postpartum depression following this second

team, and I gathered several new teammates to help my baby and me heal.

My second daughter's birth was astonishing. It was the single most transformative experience of my life, meaning I can look at my life very much in a *before* and an *after*. I didn't know I could do something so impossible: birthing my baby by myself. I couldn't believe it. And yet, I'd done it. So then I *did* believe it, because it *happened*.

My entire perception of myself shifted. It felt like such an honor to do this incredible thing. And oooooooooooh! Having done it, everything felt so different. If *this* could happen, *what couldn't?* Nothing was impossible now!

As astonishing as it was, it was also traumatizing. Very fast births often are, and they can leave the birthing person feeling vulnerable and quite fragile. Because if *this* could happen, what **couldn't?** This experience—a significant loss of control and a birth happening so very suddenly—can leave the person who gave birth feeling as if *anything* could

---

birth, particularly in the several weeks after my six-week checkup; I felt that it was time for me to get back to the real world, but I still needed more time to heal, and I was experiencing some pelvic and hip pain that had begun in pregnancy and would need longer-term care. On top of all that, my newborn daughter needed extra care for torticollis, a shortening of the muscles in her neck that prevented her from being able to turn her head to one side. To top it *all* off, when I was 11 weeks postpartum, I fell and injured my foot (the same foot I've had two surgeries on) while wearing the baby in her carrier and trying to do too much at once (Texting and walking! Don't do it!). I needed a boot and then a brace, plus physical therapy, for the next 3 months. Needless to say, it was a challenging time!

happen to them, good or bad. (Like nothing is impossible now.)

Moving through this experience and all the healing that followed it was the *definition* of vulnerabrave. In fact, it's where my usage of the term came from. It was the only thing I could come up with to describe the extremes I was feeling so deeply. Moving through this experience the way I did, all by myself (and yet definitely not alone), was a massive step on my Journey to Enoughness. It was proof positive:

I am enough.

I know, I said earlier that I learned this lesson through my healing from Catherine's death. And I did! And also: this was different. It was as if I'd scaled another peak on the Journey to Enoughness, the highest one yet; one I never saw coming but had actually been training for my entire life. The thing is, the Journey is a process of learning and re-learning that **you are Enough**, and each time, it feels different.

When the re-learning happens, it will often rock your world all over again, because it's happening at a whole new level. As you move through each of these new challenges, you'll begin embodying your enoughness in all parts of your life, and those trips to the Land of Not Enough will become not just infrequent, but nearly non-existent. And when you do go back, which you still will occasionally, it will feel like visiting a ghost town, and eventually, you'll pretty much decide to stop going there. Woot!

Perhaps I had known the truth of my enoughness in my head after healing from Catherine's death, but I had not fully *embodied* that truth yet. It wasn't until I performed an absolutely impossible task, with my own *body*, and faced one of my greatest fears at the same time (totally rocking it, I might add) that I understood. It was then that I grounded that knowing into my body and my heart.

I can do anything. **Nothing is impossible now.**

As I've processed this experience in all the time since baby girl's arrival, I've looked at our birth photos often. Four of them, taken in quick succession, in the moment right after I yelled at Leo, "GET! CAMERA!" In one, I'm reaching back to guide the baby out. In the next, her face appears for the first time. (Also there is poop in that one.) In the third, I'm holding her aloft, not unlike Simba in "The Lion King," my lips still fluttering as though in sacred song. And in the last, I'm speaking to her for the first time, welcoming her to the world.

"Hiiiiiii!"

As I look at the photos, then and now, I see my enoughness on full display. I see myself as I never did before...doing the big, impossible thing. And even if I didn't have the photos as physical proof, I feel the truth of this experience in my body. Whenever I want, I can close my eyes and take myself back to my daughter's birth, moving through that incredible process, doing the impossible, finding that it is indeed possible. Because **I am always enough.**

Don't Read the Comments

As I've mentioned more than a few times now, the Journey to Enoughness never ends. Even when we think something in our life is over, there is always more to learn from it.

For me, though the experience of birthing my second baby by myself was "over," its significance continued to unfold in every area of my life, giving me the confidence I needed to make my love of hand expression official:

131

FRANCIE WEBB

I trained as a doula. I founded TheMilkinMama. I built my business while teaching my middle school students every day. I advocated for a reduced work schedule that would allow me to spend each morning with my own children instead of other people's children. I hand expressed every three hours. I happily accepted milk from other mothers for my freezer, knowing I could use it in a bind (or on a yoga retreat), or I could pass it on to someone else in need. I purged our home of anything that didn't bring us joy, hiring someone to help me make it a place I could enjoy when I got home each day, a place where I could rest. I worked through some old hurts, by myself and with others who were involved. I told others my birth story, showing our photos to close friends, family, and strangers who were interested. I closed my eyes and relived her birth in my head.

With every new challenge that presented itself, I thought, **"You birthed a baby by yourself. You can do ANYTHING!"**

Fast forward to one year later, my second daughter's first birthday, and I felt a whisper of grief, a sense that I'd *lost* something—time? Proximity to and thus connection with my daughter's birth? Even while gaining so much. I had the sense that it had all gone by *too fast;* that the birth, and everything that happened in the year after it, were "over" in the blink of an eye. I committed to moving consciously through these feelings (and everything else I was feeling, which was a lot), not wanting to miss the beauty of the day—the beauty of celebrating this first year of my babe's life, and the one-year anniversary of the big, impossible thing I'd done.

With Leo sick in bed, it was just the girls and me at birthday dinner. I felt disappointed about that, but I also trusted that, just like the morning one year before when my birth plan imploded (and my body *ex*ploded!), things were happening for our family *exactly* as they were meant to. Dinner was great. We ordered milkshakes, sang to the birthday girl, made a video for Daddy, giggled, and took selfies.

After putting the girls to bed, and in the midst of processing the emotions of the day (pride, grief, shock, joy, and a fervent wish for time to take its time, just to name a few), I posted a heartfelt piece on a private, local Facebook group dedicated to talking about childbirth. I didn't have my husband to share my feelings with that evening, and quite frankly, I wanted to be joined in celebration.

I wanted to celebrate myself and the awesomeness with which I gave birth to my daughter. I wanted to again feel the feelings of "SEE I CAN DO ANYTHING" and to receive once again a flood of support...support I knew an authentic share would garner. I wanted to be WOWed and also to be witnessed.

I wanted to feel the feeling of birthing my own power, and to be joined in it. In empowerment.

Sharing birth photos was a normal thing in this group, so I included in my post the third of my birth photos—the one where I am receiving my daughter lovingly, *triumphantly*, into my hands. I wrote, "Today it's been one year since this happened. Where do I even begin? I am humbled. I am grateful. I am speechless. I am a badass. I am so glad my baby is one year old. And I just can't believe it." I felt proud of my Journey, and I felt a sense of closure. We had made it: through her astonishing birth and the first year of her life earthside. I put the computer to sleep with a sigh of satisfaction and relief.

Maybe half an hour later, Leo migrated from the bed to the couch, and we sat together, reflecting on this big day and the first year of our second daughter's life. You know, sitting together in the sauce:

"Look! Look what we made!"

As I was relaxing fully into gratitude, letting go of the remaining tension the conflicting emotions of the day had created inside my body, I received a jarring text from a friend. "What happened? Where did you go? I think you've been kicked out of the group and **off Facebook**!" I tried logging in. My account had been deactivated. It was as if I didn't exist anymore.

Someone. Had REPORTED. My photo.

I couldn't *believe* it.

I laughed. I felt shock and...bemusement.

"*Really?*" I thought. "*In a CHILDBIRTH group?*"

In order to reactivate my account, I had to acknowledge that I would adhere to Facebook's "Community Standards," including: **standards on *nudity***. I jumped through the hoops, went immediately to the group, and told them I was back.

Those who commented said all the "right" words of support ("Glad you're back! / I can't believe someone reported you! / Your photo is so beautiful! / Maybe it was a Facebook 'bot' that reported your photo?"), but the damage was done. After moving through the shock of what had happened, I'd begun processing a new feeling: betrayal. Who could have done this, and why? What was so triggering about the image of a woman and her baby in the act of birth? About my baby and me, doing this incredible, impossible thing?

If you haven't seen the photo (which can be found in many different places by Googling my name), I'll give you a snapshot here: I'm naked on the bed, on hands and knees, nipples exposed and pubic hair visible, holding my baby into the air, both of us still attached to a twisty blue umbilical cord that's so full of life you can almost *feel it* pulsing.

I understand that most people aren't used to seeing such "graphic" images of fellow human bodies, with the exception of seeing women's bodies being sexualized everywhere in the media for all kinds of purposes (most often to sell things or for the pleasure of another human, often a man—which is really fucked up, to be perfectly honest).[77] We are bombarded with images of boobs and near-naked bodies all day every day, but when it comes to an image of a woman giving birth, we get a little squeamish.

And yet, giving birth is one of the most basic things that we do with our bodies, *and* it's one of the most incredible. It's an act that a huge percentage of the population moves through, and one that *everyone* experiences as they come into the world.[78] The fact that birth is so stigmatized—that it remains so *hidden* in some cultures; made to seem inappropriate, almost *dirty*—that's a problem.

---

[77] As if our bodies aren't our own. Which has been exactly the experience for our brothers and sisters who suffer(ed) through slavery and oppression because of others' self-imposed power over them—and I acknowledge my privilege and fortune never to have suffered so. This legacy, of one's body being *for* others, lives on, unfortunately, in literature and advertising and social media and *even in* healthcare. We either don't have power over our own bodies, OR we *think* we don't. Either way, it's sick, and it's so very wrong.

[78] Cesarean birth is birth. Period. We are *all* birthed, each and every one of us.

FRANCIE WEBB

Why is childbirth so stigmatized? When we're talking about society at large, there are a lot of reasons. Add it to the list of potential book topics. The reason that comes up for me as it relates to my birth photo is that it can be triggering to witness another human's incredible power and deep vulnerability—both of which are fully on display when we give birth.

I know that, but I wasn't expecting to confront such discomfort or to face such *judgment*, followed by censure, in a childbirth group. I posted my photo in that group precisely because I felt safe. I felt that, out of all possible places, sharing in this group specifically, where I had seen others also post birth photos, and *where I had posted the same photo a year earlier*, would not only be safe, but it would also be considered *normal*. That I would be seen and *celebrated* for my power and vulnerabravery. That my presence would empower those who bore witness to my birth, our birth.

I quickly discovered that what I had considered a safe space actually was not safe at all.

This phenomenon—of a "safe space" suddenly becoming very unsafe—is something that most of us experience at one point or another, and if you've ever moved through it, you know how much it hurts. How confusing it is. How, even if you don't have a personal connection to the person who turned on you, it feels precisely like the deep, direct betrayal of a trusted friend. I wanted to believe that maybe it *had* been a Facebook bot that reported the photo, but I quickly confirmed that it wasn't: it was an actual member of the group.

As I continued to unpack the situation, I wondered exactly how and why my photo had been so triggering. Perhaps the person who reported me had an experience giving birth that was traumatic: maybe they had an emergency Cesarean; maybe there was something wrong with their baby's cord; maybe they had lost a child; or maybe my nakedness triggered their own body shame—shame modeled powerfully for them in our society and perfected through years of personal practice. Whatever the case, seeing my photo was triggering.

And so, they reported me, and my photo was removed. I was punished.

Excommunicated.

At least until I *promised* (to Facebook) that I would *never* do such a thing again. I did this grudgingly, to say the least.

As I got into bed that night, I wasn't sure what to think or how to feel. I'd been on such a high after celebrating my sweet babe's first birthday and after sharing my story so bravely and openly in the "safe" Facebook group. And now *this?* THIS left me stuck in the middle. In some unknown territory between self-pride and...was it **shame**?[79]

I didn't feel *ashamed*. But I did feel confused. And this particular confusion felt a lot like shame. It carried the question, "Have I done something wrong?"

---

[79] Oh, shame. I have so much I want to say about it, much of which may want to go into my next book. Much to learn, and much to teach. For now, I want to tell you that Brené Brown's work, especially her book *Rising Strong*, is the best resource I know about shame. And *my* feeling on shame is that it is *pain*. When we feel it, we don't see ourselves as worthy of others' love and connection. And we *are*. Because **we are enough.**

FRANCIE WEBB

The next morning, something major happened: I received an email from an administrator of the group, asking if I'd be willing to share my story publicly. It turned out that another member of the childbirth group, Laura, was a writer for *New York Magazine*, and that she, already feeling concerned about Facebook's policy around birth photos, wanted to hear about my experience. I agreed to speak with her. We scheduled a time for later that day.

As we were wrapping up our conversation, Laura asked, "Would you and your husband be comfortable with us publishing your photo?"

WHOA.

I hadn't thought about that.

I mean, I had, kind of: I figured that if a reporter wanted to talk about a controversial photo, they would want to show said photo. But I hadn't yet fully considered what it might be like to show *our photo* to the whole world. Right then. It felt so *sudden*. Just like baby girl's entrance into the world, a tornado of sensation I wasn't sure I could handle.

The truth is: I'd known since that photo was taken that I would publish it one day. Leo showed it to me on the bed after the baby arrived, and I knew it was special. Meant to be shared. I figured I'd share it on my blog, when I felt ready— potentially *years* down the line. I imagined it making the small-ish rounds on the internet among people who are interested in birth and babies and congregate in specialty groups (you know, like the one I posted it in). In other words, I thought I'd have some power and *control* over who saw it, and when. But THIS was a whole different ball game.

I also knew that if I gave *New York Magazine* permission to use that photo, I'd have *zero* control. That *everyone might* see it. People who know me; people who don't. People who'd be triggered by it; people who'd be empowered. If *New York Magazine* published it—if I said yes—*thousands* of people would see me in the most vulnerabrave act of my life. Also, they'd *all* see me naked. (Not the hugest deal, but also, for most of us, a pretty huge deal!)

I knew that I would have no control over how those thousands of people would receive me. That, just like in the Facebook debacle, there was a chance that people I'd felt safe with, and even people I'd never met, would excommunicate me. And that it would hurt.

Even more than that, I knew that if I said yes, *my whole life would change.* Again.

One year after my (daughter's) astonishing birth, I already had a nagging feeling that I was meant to make another big leap, and soon. That I was ready for another astonishing, life-changing experience. And at the same time, I wasn't sure I felt ready. I was afraid.

I talked with Leo. I called my principal.

I gave it some time (which, in today's world, means hours, not days).

I imagined my whole life changing: rising to fame instantly, being invited to all the talk shows, getting a book deal, and never having to work again a day in my life.[80] I also imagined

---

[80] This hypothetical sequence of events ending with "never having to work again" is particularly hilarious to me now that I have engaged in the all-consuming task of writing a book

the other way: someone using our photograph for porn, being stalked, endangering my family.

I breathed through the fear of others' self-judgment that would be projected onto me, and through the fear of facing my own self-judgment if all this backfired. I breathed through the fear that I would soon wholeheartedly regret sharing something so intimate—*so wholehearted*—with the world.

I feared that if something bad happened as a result of my vulnerabravery, it would be my fault.

Not Enough. I knew I didn't belong there anymore, and yet, there I was.

Do you see how the journey never ends? Just when you think you know you're enough—after you've done the big, impossible thing and you're vulnerabrave enough to share your power with the world—something comes along and challenges you, and you go right back to Not Enough. And you're like, "Why am I here?! I thought I was done with this!"

And in truth, you **are** done with it. At the same time, we must make that choice—to live in our Enoughness—over and over again. This is why challenges come along: to remind us of what it felt like when we were living in Not Enough, thereby propelling us forward. (Anything you've gotta do to get outta there, right?!)

(and planning for another) over the course of a year, all while working in many other capacities (doula, teacher, curriculum writer, lactation consultant-in-training, business owner, mom) as well! Writing a book is *no* vacation. To me, it actually feels more like the weeks leading up to baby's arrival, combined with the actual labor and birth process!

140

As I continued to deepen into my fear of being seen by the world, I realized that despite some of the things I'd valiantly added to my life in the year since the birth, and despite how hard I'd advocated for my own dreams, there was still so much I hadn't let go of. And as I pondered the possibilities of sharing my story *with the whole world,* I started to wonder: if *everything* had changed when I did the big, impossible thing, why did my day-to-day life still look so much the same as it had before?

I'd moved in the direction of my dreams—my doula work and TheMilkinMama were a reality—but I hadn't fully taken the leap. I was still clinging to my old life, even as I felt called to another one. I felt as if I was living a double life, or perhaps half a life?

As I pondered whether or not to share my story and my *self* with the world, I felt all of this. I felt the weight of all I'd been holding onto in my life, and it was a LOT. I realized I'd been waiting for something. I'd been waiting for a net.[81]

When Laura from *New York Magazine* asked if she could publish my photo, I realized that this was as good a net as any, if you could call it that. Regardless, I knew it was time. Time to show the world what I'd done. Time to leap into the awesome unknown that was to be the rest of my life—my new "after."

I let go.

---

[81] One of my favorite quotes is "Leap and the net will appear." It's attributed to naturalist John Burroughs. I think I first saw these words on a greeting card, and they've been serving me beautifully ever since!

FRANCIE WEBB

I surrendered to the power of birth and to the power of this experience that had been gifted to me. I felt in my body what a true honor it had been to birth my daughter, and I reminded myself of how much it had changed my whole life. Of how proud I was. How grateful I was. I knew that sharing my story at this level would change the course of my life. I considered the possibility that it would changes other's lives, too.

I said YES.

"Yes. You can share this—*the most transformative moment of my life*—with the world."

The next morning, as I made my way to school, I texted my wise friend Marisa, one of the friends who'd planned to attend my birth (and whose birth I later attended as a doula!), about my fears. About what could happen later that day, when the story went live.

"What are you afraid of?" she asked me.

"I don't know who I'm going to be after I share this photo with the world."

"You." She responded. "You will be you."

Feeling soothed, as if she'd just said "**You are enough**" (which, really, she *had*), I put away my phone. I walked into school, ready to start the day, open to all the teaching and all the learning that was to come.

New York Magazine's The Cut published the story and accompanying photo later that afternoon, just as my students were entering our classroom for the final period. Four hours after posting, the first email arrived, from *Cosmo. (Cosmo!)*

Over the next week, my inbox was filled with inquiries from nearly every online magazine I'd ever heard of, and many I hadn't: *Mashable, Huff Post, Daily Mail, SELF, Refinery 29, Pop Sugar, SheKnows, Mom.me, Yahoo News, Telemundo,* parenting and style websites and magazines from all over the world... Australia, Italy, Germany.

I went viral.

The ladies on *The View* discussed me, without using my name or showing the photo. I received messages from two popular morning shows, asking if I'd be willing to come on, but both ultimately passed because they couldn't get around the fact that *we can't show THAT on television.* Ten days after the photo was published, my sister-in-law's elderly parents walked into their local hospital (in Bergamot, Italy) and saw my photo on the wall! In a hospital! In Italy! (I still don't know why it was there or who put it there, but they called to tell her, and she told me!)

I learned quickly that I needed to get back to reporters' inquiries pronto, or else they'd publish the photo (and write their version of my story), without my permission (or any fact checking). I also made the biggest mistake one can make when a photo of you goes viral:

I read the comments.

In the first few days, I read all of them. Every word.

This is part of the Journey to Enoughness that I want to really highlight to you: people will ALWAYS have *all kinds* of opinions about who **you** are and what **you** do. And as you stand more strongly and assuredly in the truth of your enoughness, as you stand in your truth and your empowerment, oh Lord, will you have *haters.*

143

FRANCIE WEBB

And it doesn't matter.

Why?

Because **they are not *you*.**[82]

Do you know what people said about me? Some people said it was a beautiful photo: inspiring, astonishing, iconic, even. Many, many others spoke far less kindly. They said: "She looks like a man," "oh look—another attention-seeker," "no one needs to see that," "I am glad FB took it off," "that lamp is ugly."

My LAMP.

(For the record, I love that lamp! It's sitting right next to me as I type this!)

Some people wrote to me privately, leading with "Your photo is so beautiful," then moving right into, "but that's the kind of thing that should be shared in private circles, with close friends and family, only. Just my opinion. Wish you the best!" You know these people. Well-meaning haters. People who compliment you on who you are while simultaneously shaming you for what *they* believe *you've* done wrong. They're somehow triggered by what you've *done*—so much so that they want to connect with you, to share their own experience of being triggered by telling you how you should have handled things—and yet, they don't speak their truth clearly because they're *good people.* They don't want you *mad* at them. It's *complicated.*

---

[82] A favorite line from singer Sara Bareilles comes to mind, and pops into my head often, just when I need it: "Who cares if you disagree / You are not me / Who made you king of anything?" *So. Good.*

Regardless of how couched in well-meaning these messages are, the real message is very clear: *Shame on you.* And regardless of how grounded in enoughness one is, receiving that message is challenging. *Shame on you* never feels good.

I'm going to be real with you: I took it *all* to heart. Internalized every word. Doubted myself. Wondered if they were right. Thought it had been a mistake. Wondered if I'd ruined our lives—mine, Leo's, the kids'.

I knew that I'd made the right decision, and yet I kept reading the comments, many of which reinforced the Truth I'd worked so hard to let go of. The Truth I'd hoped I would rid myself of entirely by taking this big leap and sharing my story with the world. The Truth of my not-enoughness.

It was terrible.

Then someone (I don't remember who you were, but *thank you!*) told me to stop reading the comments. I don't know why I hadn't come to that conclusion myself, but I hadn't. It was as if I'd been addicted to others' feedback, and I couldn't see my way out of it on my own. I couldn't see how much it was hurting me to take in messages that reinforced my deepest fears. Once I stopped, *ahhhhhhhh*, that was so much better!

Luckily, throughout this entire experience, both before and after I stopped reading the comments, I had tremendous support from my family, friends, colleagues, and the team I'd gathered, which counteracted the worst of it. And after I stopped looking at them, I was able to let go of what others thought of me and shift my focus back to envisioning what my new life would be like, the one I'd be receiving now that I'd been brave enough to bare my birth, my body, and some of my soul to the world.

I got the chance to practice. I practiced coming home to enoughness by stepping into vulnerabravery, trusting myself to take the big leap, letting my team catch me and support me through, and making a decision to stop taking in messages that were catapulting me back into Not Enough.

And this, my friends, is how it goes. The Journey to Enoughness is never over. There is always more: to receive, to learn, to love, to give, to live. And all of it is a whole lot easier to move through if you don't read the comments.

There is *Always* More Where that Came From

Even though I'd extricated myself and shifted (mostly) out of the not-enough feelings that had been weighing on me when I was reading the comments (read: fully enmeshed in other people's opinions about me and my choices), something was still nagging at me. I stayed present with my feelings, and I soon realized that I needed to call on a very special member of my team for support to continue moving forward on my Journey to Enoughness.

"I need to talk to Nadine," I said to Leo.

Nadine is Catherine's mom. While we hadn't spoken for years after her daughter died, we'd reconnected when I was beginning my healing process as a young adult, and in the intervening years, she'd become very dear to me. We don't talk often, but she's a massive presence in my life. Both as I healed through the experience of Catherine's death, and in the years since, she's been someone who helps me feel— ENOUGH.

I messaged her, asking if we could talk that day. She FaceTimed me almost immediately, and I filled her in on what had been going on. We talked about the photo. I kept calling it "my naked photo."

"Stop calling it your naked photo," she said. "It's your BIRTH photo, and it's beautiful."

Empowered by her support, I spoke the truth in my heart, trusting her enough to ask for what I really needed: her permission. "Nadine, at some point, a reporter is going to ask me why this birth meant so much to me. And I'm going to need to talk about Catherine. Is that okay?" And, just as she always has since I first reached out to her to begin my healing, Nadine offered her unconditional support. "Of course. You tell your story any way you need to. We'll be right here with you the whole time."

I cried.

She reassured me.

We said

I love you.

We hung up the phone.

I decided to take the afternoon off, treating myself to my favorite place, the Korean spa, where for the first time in my entire life, I looked around and wondered if anyone would recognize me by my naked body! (Just one of the many side effects of sharing a naked photo of yourself with the whole world.) No one did. (Maybe next time!)

Three days later, I got a call from the umpteenth reporter, a woman writing for a mom blog. She was a friend of a dear friend, someone I felt I could trust. She asked me all the same questions everyone else had—What was it like to have my photo out there? How did I feel about Facebook's policy? What else was there to tell about my birth photo? I squirmed in my seat. I scratched my neck—itchiness a sure sign of anxiety in my body—and summoned my strength.

"I need to tell you the *real* story."

And I did.

I took this woman—this incredible writer, Sarah Yahr Tucker—back with me to the night Catherine died. To the phone call. To my parents telling me the news. I shared with her my conviction that Catherine's death was all my fault. I spoke about the years of guilt and judgment and shame. About the period in my life when I tucked my hurt so far down inside I could (mostly) pretend it wasn't there. I recounted my reunion with Catherine's family shortly after I finished college: my trip to England, Nadine and I sitting in her backyard, near the ivy that had been sprouted from ivy at Catherine's memorial service, her telling me, "When you have your babies, I'll be there for you." I talked about their trip to the States, years later, for my wedding, and shared the memory of their second son (their rainbow baby!)[83] playing a jumpy, cheerful number on the piano as my husband and I walked down the aisle.

I shared the story of their presence in my life. *On my team.*

Sarah and I worked on the story for weeks. I talked; she wrote; we cried; I talked more; she kept writing. Eventually,

---

[83] A rainbow baby is a baby born to a family after they've experienced infant loss such as miscarriage, stillbirth, or infant death.

she pitched the piece to a number of publications, most of whom turned it down.

"Too heavy," they said.

Finally, we received a YES. From *Elle*. They wanted to publish it digitally, with a number of revisions that neither Sarah nor I really wanted to make. But we were eager to see the story out there in the world, so Sarah made the changes, and they published it—finally, the day before my 35th birthday.

And then, do you know what happened?

The haters STOPPED.

Not completely—there was, and still is, the rare moment when someone says a 14-year-old should never have been caring for an infant or comes across my birth photo and leaves a nasty comment (not that I read them)—but for the most part, they stopped. In place of their comments came two things: 1. Words of love and support from all over the world, and 2. *Silence.*

And I learned so much from this. Because true, deep healing, and deciding that **we are the most important person** (others' perceptions of us just don't *matter!*) changes us.

The thing is: Others will have their opinions. I'm not saying their opinions don't matter, ever; sometimes our teammates offer us their truth about our experiences, to our benefit and theirs. But most of the time, if you are like me and you can tell that you've cared too much about what others think of you, for *far* too long, **YGTD** to care less about what they think, and care the MOST about what YOU think.

Sometimes, the thing we need to remember above all else is that it's best not to read the comments!

Am I Doing This Right?

We hear this question all the time. From other people, yes, and also in our own heads. In fact, it's one of the questions I receive most frequently from people who discover TheMilkinMama on social media.

"I can hand express, but I'm not sure if I'm doing it right. Am I doing it right???"

This "doing it right" phenomenon goes far beyond hand expression. Most parents (most people, really) are constantly wondering if they've made the "right" decision.

Is this the right caregiver/school/outfit? Is a bib-free chocolate ice cream-eating sesh okay? Is it bad if I sit enjoying a quiet moment while my child tears up a pop-up book and throws couch cushions all over the floor? Did I make the right decision to move to part-time? Is this the best marketing strategy? What's the right way to bring in the income I need, to live the life I deserve? Should I just go back to my old job? Should I say no to this opportunity that doesn't feel like a good fit?

We spend so much time wondering if what we're doing is what we *should* be doing. Questioning whether or not we're doing it "right." We're so stuck in this idea that there is A Right Way to do things, and concomitantly (I love that word *soooooo* much!), we posit any way that isn't The Right Way as The Wrong Way.

Enough is enough.

It's time for those of us who haven't already, to grow out of this. To realize that this is crazy-making and that we are doing it to ourselves. That if we stop obsessing over Right and Wrong, we can rely on our enoughness to take us to new heights. We can trust ourselves and our decisions, and we can empower others to do the same.

When someone asks, "Am I doing this right?" You can say, "What do *you* think?"

Make a conscious decision to invite them into the process of seeking their own truth—discovering their own enoughness—rather than simply telling them what to do. This might really annoy them. Especially if they're stuck believing that there's a Right way to do things and that the answer to their problems is somewhere outside of themselves, in someone else's prescriptions or directions.

When I was a kid, my dad always answered questions with questions, which drove me crazy. Or, he'd respond to my questions with an indication that I already knew the answer to what I was asking. "You tell me," he'd say in his deep booming voice. This frustrated me so much. I was like, "I wouldn't be asking if I knew the answer!"

As I've grown up, I've come to understand that a lot of times, we think we don't know the answer, we actually do. This is true particularly when it comes to our own bodies. We live inside them, and so does our own instinct: an ancient, completely inexplicable, comprehensive **wisdom** that, if we tune into it, guides us perfectly.

I lean into this truth when people ask me, "Am I doing this right?" in reference to hand expression. Inside my head I'm screaming, "OF COURSE YOU ARE! THERE'S NO SUCH THING! WHATEVER YOU ARE DOING IS RIGHT *FOR YOU!*"

and doing a celebratory dance. I'm celebrating because regardless of how they're actually doing the thing (hand expression in this case), I know that simply by being here and having the vulnerabravery to seek guidance, they're on their Journey.

I coach them through the experience, being careful not to tell them what to do (because **they get to decide**), asking questions that will help us identify which part of what they're doing isn't working for them.

Is milk coming out?

Does it hurt?

Are you comfortable? If not, what change could you make to feel more comfortable?

Does it *feel* like it's working for you?

If the answer is "yes," then—YAY!—the answer is Yes!

If the answer is "no," then it's time to ask another question: "What can I shift to make this practice work for me?"

Because here's the truth around the Right versus Wrong way issue: in many, many life situations, perhaps most of those we will *ever* face, there is more than one way to do things. In fact, there is rarely ever a "wrong" way either. Sure, there are some ways that may have more unpleasant consequences than others, but if we're grounded in the belief that our journey is, you know, a *journey*, and that we're truly *already on* it, it's clear that there is no "wrong" decision in most cases, even if others say otherwise.

And when it comes to hand expression, it's the same. There is no right way. Instead, there are so many different ways to achieve awesome outcomes, milk-wise and otherwise. These are the ways that are a great match for *you*, and **you get to decide** what they are.

Recently, I read an article in a popular parenting website, "I Tried Hand Expression For A Week, & It Totally Sucked." I'll be honest, I didn't read it start to finish. My mind was racing as I took in this writer's experience, which was so very different from my own. But I read enough to feel a lot of feelings, since hand expression is my new life's work.

In the parts I did read, I noticed that the author tried only ONE way to hand express before she made a declaration that hand expression, as a whole, sucks.

Like the whole Wrong vs. Right epidemic, this is a problem. When we act like there is only one way to do something, we cut ourselves off from so many valid paths. We exclude so many options for approaching life. Options that might really help us if we actually took the time to investigate them.

It's time for those of us who posit ourselves as *experts* to stop pretending that there is only one way: to hand express, to be in a yoga pose, to practice self-care, to birth, to parent, to be successful, or just to *be*...on this planet. It's time for all of us to open up to the truth: there are so many valid options here. The job of the expert is only to advise, and then **you get to decide** which options to try. Further, **you get to decide** which combination of all the options works best to facilitate **your** Journey.

You also get to move through the world with the understanding that just as **you get to decide** what makes your life better / easier / more fulfilling, **others get to**

decide what works for them, and you must learn to respect those choices. Different people choosing differently isn't a bad thing. When we trust ourselves to make choices that feel good to us and trust others to do the same, allowing all choices to be considered equally valid (with the exception of those that bring harm to another, obviously)—Well. When we trust ourselves to do *that*, we have so much power. We can share our enoughness with one another. We can trust one another to be truthful about what we need, and how we feel. We can ask each other challenging questions, learning from one another, all of us becoming stronger and more compassionate as a result. When we decide for us, and others decide for them, and we share our Journeys to Enoughness with each other, *everybody wins*.

Imagine a world where each of us could try what felt good to us without wondering if we were doing it Right or Wrong. Without wondering who might be judging us for our choices. Imagine a world where every one of us had access to ALL of the options, and then we *tried them as we pleased*, persisting even with the ones that felt not-so-easy at first, until we reached mastery, or comfort, or whatever it is we are seeking.

What a badass world that would be!

So in this up-and-coming world of ours, how do you begin deciphering what it is that you really want? How do you figure out what's going to move you toward, and further along, your Journey to Enoughness?

You trust yourself to play around.

In hand expression and in *all* areas of your life, trust yourself to play around. You'll quickly find that you have everything you need, right inside yourself, and although you'll rely on your team to continue on your journey, you'll realize you *can* do the impossible. Always and in all ways.

You've got this.

When you feel alone, go inside your body. Find a place and space where you can get quiet, be still, and ask, "What do I need right now?" Wait for the answer—seconds, minutes, however long it takes. The more you stay open to the answer, the more clearly it will come.[84]

Also, read this book. The one that's in your hands right now. Reread it, too. Repeat to yourself: **I am never alone.** Make it your mantra, for the next minute or hour or day or week. Reach out to a member of your team and tell them how you feel. Then receive their support, support you've cultivated your*self* by choosing them, oh so brilliantly, for your team.

Remember, great support should never make you feel not-enough. If you're seeking support and you feel great receiving it, GREAT. If you don't, that's not true support. It may be time to switch-up your line-up of experts, or simply to reach out to a different teammate for support. If you're not sure who to reach out to, try us. Even if your question isn't about hand expression specifically, we may be able to direct you to a resource for what you're working with.

That's one of the ways I aim for TheMilkinMama to be different than other resources you can find for support with hand expressing and feeding your baby. Whether you read this book, check out a video, take a Go Milk Yourself

---

[84] Isn't it amazing how we can be by ourselves, yet not alone at all? And that sometimes, we need to go be by ourselves to realize that **we are never alone**?

workshop, book a private session, attend an event, connect on social media, shoot us an email when you're having a meltdown on your pump break, or any combination of these: I want you to know that we're here for you. **You are never alone.** You have us, people you may not know from Adam but who are rooting for you every step of the way. And, unlike many other times in life when we have invisible cheerleaders, we're cheerleaders you can reach out to and get an answer.

We're here for you, because we at TheMilkinMama believe that humans are meant to help one another.

Chapter 8:
But What If...?
(Frequently Asked Questions About Hand Expression)

Why should I hand express? Is it better than pumping?
I'm not saying you "should" hand express or that hand expression is better than pumping. I'm saying it's a great option. It can make your life easier. You might get more milk. You may find yourself less stressed when you're in a bind. It's a practice that can empower you to do things you currently believe you cannot do. **You get to decide.** When it comes to getting your milk out, any way that works for you is valid.

For me, hand expression quickly replaced pumping, which I hated. Even though it probably was working just fine for me, I perceived "not enough" with pumping, even though I really had totally normal and healthy output. (For more on this phenomenon of "not enough," see Chapters 6 and 7.)

The thing is, if you take the time to learn and practice hand expression, you'll be able to decide what's "better" for you and when to use which option. You may decide that one is better than the other; you may not. And you might decide that using both, in addition to nursing (if you are doing that), is the best option. The bottom line, as always: **YGTD.**

FRANCIE WEBB

Other than the obvious fact that you're using your hands instead of a machine, is there any difference between hand expression and pumping in terms of how it works?
Hand expression does offer two different types of pressure, which most pumps do not. Most pumps operate only by negative pressure, which indicates an object pulling another object away from its environment, like a pump pulling the breast away from the chest wall. When an object is being pushed into, like the action of a baby's mouth and tongue against the breast, that's positive pressure. Unlike most pumps, your hands can create both negative pressure (by pulling the breast away from the chest wall to get a grip on it) and positive pressure (by compressing your fingers and hands into the breast tissue).

In other words, hand expression can more closely replicate the hard work that babies can do with a strong latch and an agile tongue, than most pumps can.

Using your hands, you can also more easily find where in your breast the milk likes to hang out and customize your moves. With that extra feedback, which you don't get from pumping alone, you're able to get milk out from the spots where you feel more full. What's more, these may also be the places where things are more likely to get backed up, so you're more likely to detect and address problems before they occur. You can even incorporate breast self-exam practices recommended by your health care provider in to your practice. Then you'll always be able to tell if someone's awry, or all is well!

How do pumping and hand expression work together?
Pumping and hand expression go hand in hand!

You can hand express *instead* of pumping.

You can hand express *in conjunction with* pumping.

Here's one way your routine could look with an electric pump:

1. Massage before pumping.
2. Pump hands-free with a bra that your pump parts fit into.
3. Go Milk Yourself after pumping, using your compression strategies to get that "bonus" milk out.

If you are using a manual pump that has a trigger-like mechanism, you can still massage before pumping and hand express afterward.

If you have a silicone hand pump, you can use it the same way you would with the manual pump mentioned above. In addition, because it can suction to your breasts, you can attach it to one side while you hand express on the other side. Because letdown on one side encourages letdown on the other side, you may find that the milk just falls into the silicone pump while you're working on Go Milk Yourself next door. Then you can switch sides.

Should I get a manual pump?
I mean, you have one. On your hands. Because MANUAL! HAHA! And in this book, you have a manual that teaches you how to Go Milk Yourself—yay!

And also: there are manual pumps that are not your hands.

Many parents love them, either instead of or in addition to an electric pump. These are usually single pumps that use either a trigger-style handle, or the silicone ones mentioned above that suction to your breast with a bulb-like bottom that you squeeze. Like I said, you can use the latter as passive pumps on one side while you nurse or hand express on the other, and if feels like milk just "falls" out. Yay milkfalls!

Any which way, it's *always* great to have options, and it's wise, too. As you already know, the one that's attached to our bodies is *my* favorite—now **YGTD**!

So can I dump the pump?

Just as my dad would, I'm going to answer this question with a question:

Would you *like* to stop pumping?

If you're determined to live a pump-free life, I believe that you can. **Gather your team**, commit to practicing, and give it a go. Reach out for support anytime you need.

My pump is working great for me. How can hand expression help someone like me?

First of all, GO YOU. I'm so pumped that you and your pump have a fab relationship. You deserve that, *and* I know it makes your life easier. So YAY!

Second, there are two ways that learning to Go Milk Yourself can help you:
1. You'll be less stressed when you get into a bind and aren't able to pump, and
2. You may be able to get more milk out than with pumping only.

In summary, hand expression can help you because it gives you more freedom and more power!

How does hand expression "give me more freedom"?
Of course, the answer to this question all depends on what freedom feels like to you.

Possible benefits to hand expression instead of pumping include fewer parts to wash, more time (since you don't have to set up and take down an electric pump, *plus* wash all those parts), a greater sense of connection with your body, and the ability to just carry a bottle in your bag rather than the whole pump. This last piece can be particularly helpful on a date night, at a wedding, on a work trip, or when attending any event that keeps you from baby for a number of hours. Some newer pumps are designed to be smaller, so that's a win for those of you who'd feel better having an electric pump with you, and manual pumps, especially the silicone ones, don't take up a lot of space. Just remember that you don't *need* to schlep a pump wherever you go, because you've got one right there on your own body, at the ends of your arms.

One con to hand expression is that you can't do it hands-free. Because then it would just be expression, which means a whole lot of other things. And if you, like Roald Dahl's Matilda, can find a way to get your milk out through sheer will, more power to you. And please share!

But I thought hand expression was only for emergencies.
In that case, you're already ahead of where I was, because I didn't even know it existed! It's fascinating to me that we think we should only use this particular tool that's built into our bodies, when we're desperate. What does that say about us? A LOT! What if, instead, we became experts at this tool

that's right at the end of our arms, and then used it to support us *whenever we decided to*? Talk about power. So now, hand expression isn't just for emergencies. That said, knowing how to Go Milk Yourself will make any "emergency" that comes up, feel more like no big deal!

How is hand expression different than if I just squeeze my breast and milk comes out?

This question was on a recent survey we sent when I really jumped back in to this book, and I have to say, I LOVE IT SO MUCH. Because, it's *not* different from that. Not really. And I can tell that the asker of this question is also a knower of their own body. <fist bump emoji> GO YOU!!! If you can squeeze[85] your breast and milk comes out, go go go. You've got this. You may still find some helpful information within the Go Milk Yourself Method. And you may not need any extra instruction at all. Any which way, we're happy you're doing this with us, here on this planet, because the more each of us finds power within our own bodies, the more likely we are to use that power to serve others, in exactly the ways we are meant to.

How do you do it other than just squeezing the crap out of your boobs?

Please don't squeeze the crap out of your boobs! That'd hurt. You can do real damage. (Plus, you don't have crap in your boobs—you have precious milk!) Go Milk Yourself; don't hurt yourself. Refer to Chapter 5 for the moves that'll get your

---

[85] Though I usually don't use this word, I've decided that "squeeze" is okay here. Because, although I believe in precise language, it's consistent with the language used by the person who asked this question, and it seems to work great for them!

milk movin'. And, as always, reach out to TheMilkinMama anytime you need support!

Does hand expression hurt?

The short answer is no, not usually. The longer answer is that, just like in the rest of your body, you may experience pain in your breast, chest, or hands when hand expressing. Such pain can be a sign that's something's out of whack. If you are experiencing pain while hand expressing, nursing, and/or pumping, please, I beg you, find a lactation professional who can help you initiate, continue, or wind down lactation. Don't just choose the first one you hear about or the most convenient one to meet with; find an awesome lactation professional. Trust your gut over anyone else's advice for you—**you are your own expert.** And always, always consult with your team[86] to determine the cause of the pain, work to relieve it, and get long-term support no matter what next steps feel best in your lactation journey. Pain, in any area of our bodies and lives, may be a sign that something needs changing. It's always worth addressing.

Aren't I supposed to press my breast back into my chest wall?

First of all, there's no "supposed to" in this work, because **you get to decide.** It's *your* body you're working with. A lot of instruction you'll find on the internet, and from hospital staff and lactation professionals, will include this move. It's not part of my repertoire or what I teach—I don't go in thinking, "I'm going to press my breast back into my chest wall," and teach others to do the same. Instead, I go in

---

[86] Medical providers, lactation support professionals, best friends, partners, fellow parents, other loved ones and experts who are actually helpful. The list goes on.

thinking, "Let me get this milk out, and let me stay comfortable while doing it." And then I express. And it works! All that said, I *do* notice that once I'm set up to hand express the way I know how, I sometimes press my breast back while moving like me. So, you might press your breast back into your chest wall. But you don't have to. **YGTD!**

When are the best times to hand express?
You know what I'm going to say first, right?

You get to decide!

And

There's no wrong answer.

Looking for a bit more structure? Here are some specific suggestions:

The following times can be great times to Go Milk Yourself:
1.   Right after pumping.
2.   Every 3ish hours when away from baby .
3.   When baby sleeps longer than expected **and** you'd like to get some extra milk for your stash.
4.   When you are relaxed and distracted (i.e. catching up on your favorite series and baby is sleeping).
5.   When you're on the toilet *as long as your hands are clean.*[87]

---

[87] You're relaxed, gravity is on your side, you're staying put for a hot minute, and you *might* have a moment to yourself (or you might have one or more pairs of eyeballs belonging to pets or children staring at you). Credit for this suggestion goes to the great Andrea Syms-Brown.

How long will it take me to hand express?
I can't say. But you can! Try the moves in this book, reach out for support, and you'll soon know about how much time it takes you to complete a hand expression session, whatever that means to you.

I used to pump for half an hour. When I first started to hand express at work, I set aside thirty minutes and realized it probably took me about twenty. By the time my second baby was about 5 months old, I was setting aside 20 minutes for hand expression sessions at work, and I would estimate that 8-13 minutes of it was active hand expression. The rest was breaks, answering an email or two, going to the bathroom, washing my hands, etc.

I can give you these examples from my own life, but only you can answer this question. In fact, once you've mastered it, I'd love to hear from you: How long does it take *you* to Go Milk Yourself?

How much milk will I get?
I can't say. As with pumping, your output depends on so many things, including: how full you are, how much baby took from the tap in the last nursing session, whether you're hand expressing by itself or after pumping, if you're stressed or relaxed...you name it. When I was expressing around the clock at work, I was able to get about enough for a full feeding in the 8-13 minutes I mentioned above.

Whatever your output, remember that **you are enough**, and **you are never alone**. Reach out to us at info @themilkinmama.com anytime to share how it's going for you. We're here to help.

FRANCIE WEBB

I'm hand expressing, but I'm getting milk all over my hands/laps/clothes/screen. Is this normal? What can I do about it?

Much like life, hand expression can be a messy process, and just because you get better at it doesn't necessarily mean you'll always make less of a mess. Using a wider-mouthed vessel can help; that way you can catch all the sprays, drips, drops, and even milkfalls, no matter the direction they're headed (and sometimes they're much like fireworks!). Remember that the flange/breastshield of a pump has a funnel shape and can also help catch those rogue (read: badass!) sprays.

You can change your positioning as well, leaning forward or back, still keeping your shoulders down, and that may help. If you're getting it on your hands, I always say not to stress too much. No stress when you express, even when it's a mess, that's my motto!

Get the milk that you can, from the most relaxed state available to you. If you're worried about the milk that you're "losing" when things make a mess, remember: **There's more where that came from**. And there are always towels for your lap, hands, computer screen, and anything else in the line of milk-fire. (My friend had drops of my milk on the dash of her Prius for a long time after our last yoga retreat, which I found hilarious—and luckily, she did too!)

I'll also mention that when I express in a private space, I usually take off my entire shirt or dress. It's just easier, and then I don't have to worry about popping back in to a classroom or client meeting with mysterious wet spots all over my clothes.

I'm only getting drips and drops when I hand express. Is this normal?
First of all, notice when you use the word *only* to describe your milk, and your self. Remember that **you are enough**, and shift your language so that it reflects this truth. Your milk is awesome, and so are you.

Second: The vast majority of people we have taught to hand express begin their practice with drips and drops. Over time, most are able to see sprays and streams for at least a portion of their hand expressing time, and some see *mostly* sprays and streams after they've had a bit of practice. If you are hand expressing and notice that things slow down—turning from sprays and streams to drips and drops—stop and massage, and then compress again. If you get a steady drip, and that seems to be working well for you, you can always use the Press and Hold to offer that milk a steady hand on its journey into the outside world. You can do this. If you need help, please ask. **You are never alone.**

I keep getting clogged ducts and mastitis. Can hand expression help?
As a rule, clogged ducts and mastitis are caused by inefficient milk removal, which is when milk isn't coming out at a rate that matches the needs of the parent's body. In some cases, this may be related to overproduction of milk, which can occur when milk is produced at a rate so fast that the ducts that lead to the nipples cannot drain. Hand expression may help, because it allows you to reach areas of the breast that a pump cannot. If you are having these (or any other breastfeeding) problems, and you are not already under the

care of an awesome lactation professional,[88] please consider finding one so that you can get the support you need. The support that you deserve! **You are never alone.**

For some people, pumping can exacerbate clogged ducts and mastitis rather than helping them. If this is true for you (and again, you and your ALP can work this out), adding hand expression to your nursing and/or pumping repertoire could help.

Any way you squeeze it, it's important to get to the root cause of the challenges you're having. What is causing this less-than-optimal removal of milk? Ask yourself this, find your ALP, and use your team to find the answers and decide what's next. You can do it!

When is the best time to learn to hand express?
How about now?! You can learn to hand express whenever you want. Our workshops are open to parents and expectant parents, and we believe that learning *before* baby comes out can be helpful because then you'll have this tool to use in the early postpartum days, when scheduling *anything* can be a challenge. If you need support deciding when to take a

---

[88] Because I'm going to reference this magical, yet very real, provider (member of your TEAM!) a number of times in this section, I'll go ahead and abbreviate this phrase. Awesome Lactation Professional (ALP): n., someone who is trained in lactation, knows their stuff, truly hears you and respects you, gives you "You can do it" vibes rather than "You're doing it wrong" ones, and offers EITHER built-in follow-up, like phone calls, emails, video check-ins, texts, and support groups, and/or refers you to someone who can. Once you've found an ALP, you should never be alone.

workshop or private session, just reach out—we are here for you!

How early is it safe to hand express? Can I do it while pregnant?
Ask your team (doctor + lactation consultant + others you trust) this question. We'll teach you whenever you want; **you get to decide** the when.

What if hand expression stresses me out?
If you're hand expressing and you hear all kinds of voices in your head that feel like scarcity and anxiety, do something to relax your self. Stop, close your eyes, breathe. Tell yourself something awesome. I like to talk to myself as I would to my children, saying things like, "It's okay, sweet girl. I'm right here with you. You're doing great." Regardless of what kind of self-talk feels most powerful to you, a moment of conscious pause[89] can make a big difference.

So can walking away.

If you're just learning, and you find yourself all worked up, my recommendation is to walk away. You can always come back later, when you're more relaxed. And if you're stressed because you're in a serious need-to-get-milk-out situation, that's a great moment to reach out for help. Reach out to

---

[89] The concept of "conscious pause" was taught to me by Erich Schiffmann, the great yoga and meditation teacher. He says we can take a moment to come back to ourselves, to peace and calm and knowing that we are enough, really, whenever we want, and that the more we practice this, the better we'll get, and we'll start living our whole lives more consciously.

someone on your team or ours! You can find videos and other helpful resources at www.themilkinmama.com.

Any tips for getting over the fear of getting started?

A dear friend and mentor of mine, Dana Fotiades, tells me: "Everything you want is on the other side of fear." I love that saying. To me, it means: "You can still do the thing you *really want* to do. Even if you're afraid. And getting through that fear—really working with it, not fighting it but learning from it instead—is The Way to get to where you want to be."

In short, it means: YOU CAN DO IT, and **you get to decide** the when and the how.

To get over your fear of getting starting with hand expression, my first tip would be to read this book in its entirety, if you haven't already. I hope you'll then realize that moving through that fear in whatever way you'd like (breezing right past it, bulldozing through it, or anywhere in between) will be worth any time and energy you decide to invest.

Seriously, though. What if I'm like, *really* afraid to start?

Each of our emotions (and, I believe, experiences) has a purpose. Fear has a purpose. The purpose of fear is often to protect us from something undesired or painful. Maybe you're currently experiencing something undesired or straight-up painful (scarcity, anxiety, stress, pain within your body...just to name a few options). Or maybe you're needing to heal something painful from your past. Your pain might even be what brought you to this here book. (I'm so glad you're here.)

The truth is, we don't have to understand our fear to move through it. We can heal, on every level, the things that need healing in our life, by deciding to move through that fear, and just going for it. In other words, you don't to have to toss that fear out the window in order to Go Milk Yourself successfully. You can fear getting started, *while also* getting started. It's okay to both honor your fear *and* act on your desire to get started, as paradoxical as those two things may feel—in fact, we do this often, in our bodies and in our lives. So, you can do it. Today, tomorrow, or any other day you choose.

You are the most important person. When you ask for and receive the help that you need, everyone benefits. So, moving through this fear is worth it!

A few options for getting over *any* fear are:
1. Talk to someone you love. Someone who you know really sees and hears you. Tell them the biggest fear you're feeling right now. Tell them what you hope to do and share with them how they can support you. Be honest with them about what you need. Agree to let them know how it goes. #accountability
2. Try whatever it is you're afraid to do with a friend. It's great to have a partner!
3. Relax. Do something funny or relaxing right before doing the scary thing, or while doing it.
4. Go inside yourself, get quiet, be still. This might be meditation, guided relaxation, a long hot bath, bodywork, you name it. Practice this. Get good at it. You'll figure out what's YOU and what's just noise. Then, when you do the thing you're afraid of, you'll be better able to identify what's present for you, and to differentiate between limiting beliefs and your truth (which is always: You can do it!).

5. As my mom would say, "Get over it." As my sister would say, "Cut down a tree, build a bridge, and get over it." I don't love it when people say such things to me (sorry, Mom and Sister), and yet, "get over it" is sometimes exactly what we need to hear. Because what people are really saying, when they say "get over it" is "just go!" It's like that time I thought I couldn't ride a bike without training wheels until my (younger) brother put me on one, gave me a shove, and yelled, "JUST!!! PEDALLLLLLLLLL!!!" And I did. And it worked![90]

Can someone else hand express for me?

The short answer is yes. With your permission (your body, so **YGTD**), your partner or nurse or doula or child or lactation consultant or helpful family member can massage and compress your breasts or chest. This can be particularly effective when you're in pain and it's hard to touch your own body. I've seen a very experienced doula in South Korea take a hot wet towel and use it to help a mother whose milk had just come in get a bit of relief from fullness. All that said, we believe that nobody knows your body (and your SELF!) better than you, so setting yourself to be the #1, go-to, VIP hand expresser of your own milk is important.

Can I express into the same container of milk, more than once?

You can hand express into the same milk you already hand expressed, as long as it's room temperature. Combining milk at the same temperature is safe. Latest estimates show milk

---

[90] I was nine at the time. He was six. I was really, really afraid of riding without training wheels. But then I did it! And I loved it! #storyofmylife

can stay at room temperature between 10 and 24 hours. You can find many reliable sources about milk storage on the internet. **You get to decide** what's comfortable for you—and you can *always* smell and taste your milk to determine if it's still good for your baby. Much like grown-up humans, small ones will reject spoiled food.

Can I feed my baby with breast milk and supplement with formula?
Of course you can! **You get to decide**!

What if somebody makes a recommendation I'm not comfortable with?
If you've read the **Gather Your Team** section in Chapter 7 of this book, the answer to this question is easy: find someone else on your team you can ask, or seek out a new member of your team for a second opinion. And if you haven't, now's a good time to check it out. My dear friend Samantha said recently, "The most important thing is that you are informed and comfortable." If you find that you are neither of these, or just one of the two, work to get what you need until you are both.

This is what it means to **be your own expert**—become the expert at getting what you need.

You deserve it.

Tell me about the research on hand expression, please.
There are two well-known studies that explore hand expression. They were both conducted by the University of California San Francisco. You can visit the Resources page on our website OR do a quick Google search to find them.

In one, 68 mothers whose babies struggled to latch in the first 3 days of life were assigned either to pumping or hand expression and taught their respective method of milk removal. Of the mothers in the group, 97 percent of mothers in the hand expression group were still breastfeeding two months after birth, and 72 percent of others in pumping group were still breastfeeding two months after birth.

In the other, 21 mothers were studied in the first 3 days of their baby's lives. They were assigned to express breastmilk by pumping and then hand expressing or hand expressing and then pumping. The components of their milk were then analyzed. The fat contents of the hand-expressed milk were found to be higher than that of pumped milk, and the conclusion was that massage was the key to yielding this fattier milk. And if you didn't know already, fatty milk is #goals when it comes to feeding babies!

It's worth noting that a lot of the research out there fails to mention hand expression as an option for lactating parents. I read something recently that basically said, "It's clear that if you're not nursing and you want to keep up your milk production, you must pump." I disagree. Because—yay!—you can Go Milk Yourself instead. Having options is the breast!

Do I *really* need a lactation consultant or counselor? Can't I just ask my doctor what to do?

A lactation professional is trained in *lactation,* which is the process by which a parent makes milk in their body for their child(ren). This is the first reason why, if you're having any issues with said process, you really need a lactation consultant, and an AWESOME one. (I mean, **YGTD.** AND: I highly, highly recommend you find a real expert to assist you, someone you connect with who knows things that you don't yet know.)

Doctors are trained in their specialty, which might be general medicine, obstetrics and gynecology, pediatrics, or many other options. Even if you're seeing someone who's meant to care for you and your baby during pregnancy and the postpartum period, they may not have lactation training. In fact, rare is the doctor who has lactation training. Did you know that the breasts are the only part of our bodies that don't have their own medical specialty? There *are* doctors of breastfeeding medicine, and many are awesome, but they are few and far between. In addition, many are sought for significant breastfeeding problems rather than general support and preventative care. If you do find a doctor with lactation training, and s/he feels like a good fit all around, you've basically hit the lottery!

Let me also remind you that a doctor effectively diagnosed me with low milk supply, and recommended that I feed my baby formula when I really didn't want to, when lactation support was really outside her scope.

Some pediatricians, and other doctors, are trained lactation consultants. Most aren't. Choose doctors, and other providers, you trust to care for you and your child(ren). These people will become part of your *team*. Be discerning. You'll know whom to ask for what.

Bottom Line: If you want to breastfeed or chestfeed your child(ren), I urge you to find an ALP. Ideally, you'd meet this person before your baby arrives, perhaps in a breastfeeding (and/or hand expression!) class.[91] That way, you'll have your

---

[91] At the time of this writing, online Go Milk Yourself workshops take place with MilkinMama teachers twice a month. Private sessions are available daily. If you can't find someone local, we can offer you support via phone or

ALP's contact information, and more important, a relationship with her or them, so you can reach out as soon as you have a question or need support. *Or* they can refer you to someone who is available when they are not. Any which way, get help, and you'll be glad.

Why not just learn on YouTube?
Learning anything online, and for free, from the comfort of your very own couch/pumping room/private jet, is a pretty fab option. There are thousands of free videos on YouTube (and elsewhere) that demonstrate hand expression. Use them! You'll know if something's helpful, and you'll definitely know if it's not.

And in a related question...

How is the Go Milk Yourself Method different from other ways of teaching hand expression?
Here are a few reasons. The rest you may find for yourself as you practice many of the moves on our menu of options.

- o We're like really, *legit* here for you. In person, on video chat, at the other end of the phone or a text, on social media, ready to receive and respond to your email.
- o At TheMilkinMama, rather than demonstrating *one* way to hand express, we give you options. A whole menu of them. We teach them to you live, offering you time to troubleshoot all your new tricks. And then we support you after you learn. That's our method—it's continuous care with real people who, you know, *care*.

---

computer. All of these resources are open to pregnant and lactating parents.

o We not have only a demo; we have a whole curriculum, and a pedagogy, too.[92] We hope this means that hand expression feels accessible to you, and that you will thus be more willing to try it, practice it, and share your findings with us and others, to the benefit of all.

o We also have trained ALPs available to support you with needs beyond hand expression. If you need help on short notice, and you can't find someone local to you, or it just makes your life that much easier to get help virtually, we can find someone for you before you can say "boobs" (well, maybe slightly longer than that).

o As a rule, you pay for our services. *What, Francie? Did you just say that? Is that supposed to be a pro? Because it sounds like a con!* We do charge for workshops, private sessions, videos, this book, and most other platforms that allow us to share what we've developed. Our team is comprised of individuals who have extensive experience with and training in hand expression. We've spent many hours together,

---

[92] Pedagogy (n.), a teacher word that means the philosophy behind how one teaches something. Your pedagogy seeps into everything you do. How you do one thing is how you do everything. If a teacher sets timers throughout a class, clearly timekeeping is an important part of her pedagogy. If she pauses after asking a question, waiting for more hands to go up, she's clearly made engagement a priority, *and* she wants to make sure that her students understand what she's asking before she moves on. If a classroom is kept organized in a way that all learners can get to the supplies they need with ease, that teacher's pedagogy includes the knowledge that space influences the learning community. At TheMilkinMama, our pedagogy is best described in our credo and tenets.

learning and growing and revising our thinking and becoming more inclusive and knowledgeable with time. Our time is valuable, so we charge for our work. We also work behind the scenes to make our instruction affordable and accessible to all. If you or someone you know wants to learn to Go Milk Yourself, and they can't afford it, please email us at info@themilkinmama.com. We will do anything we can to support you in this worthy and fulfilling endeavor. And if you would like to pay for services for someone who can't swing the cost, we welcome that with open boobs, too. No matter your circumstances, we thank you for trusting us and promise to be our best for you.

o   We offer long-term support. TheMilkinMama Support Group on Facebook is for anyone who's taken a workshop or private session, online or in-person. A prerequisite for joining is a working knowledge of the Go Milk Yourself Method, taught to you live. It also includes all of our teachers, as well as birth and lactation professionals who have taken our workshops. We offer online Q&As (we call them Breast Conferences) so that participants can get questions answered in real time by MilkinMama teacher. Our group is a great place (perhaps the breast!) to ask questions, troubleshoot your practice, share pictures of your milk, pump each other up, celebrate accomplishments, get camaraderie in the toughest moments—you name it. That's a 24/7 thing, because, you know, Facebook—plus, when you gather parents and birth professionals in a group, someone's always awake!

When it comes to support for hand expression, no one else offers what we do.

So if you find yourself asking, "Why should I pay these people to learn this thing I can find for free on YouTube?"

Now you have *my* answer. **You get to decide** what to do with it!

Remind me again why I should hand express.

Because it's awesome and badass and empowering and gratifying and YOU CAN DO IT!

Chapter 9:
The Most Frequently Asked Question of All

You've reached the conclusion of this book, and the place where I'll answer the most frequently asked question I receive, and the one I have asked myself more times than any other:

What does Go Milk Yourself MEAN?
Go Milk Yourself means:
1. Learn to hand express
2. Get good at it
3. Recognize that this is a powerful act, *and* an act of power
4. Use it to help you
5. Use it to help others.

I want you, reader, helper, **most important person,** to Go Milk Yourself. And that doesn't just mean getting milk out of your boobs, breasts, or chest. I want you to discover this thing you can do that you thought you couldn't. I want you to discover that you can do it all by yourself, with your own damn power. That you were born with this power and **you are enough. With practice, you have *even more* power, and it's all in your hands.**

And then I want you to let the biological process of lactation be a model for you of what's possible in the rest of your life— in your body, in your work, in how you choose to spend your time, in your relationships, in your impact on this world. **Be your own expert** on your self. Because with your milk, your power, and your badass self, **there's *always* more where that came from**.

FRANCIE WEBB

This biological process of "my body knows what to do" is the same as "I know what to do." There's a big level of trust here: "I was made to do this. I was *born* to do this." These are facts about each of us. Even though we don't always *think* we know how. Even though it seems preposterous at times—it might even seem preposterous right this second—**we can do the impossible thing**. We already do. All of us. Every day. And we aren't going it alone—in fact, **we are never alone**. So please, give your self permission, and **gather your team**.

The truth is: you can let Go Milk Yourself be the inspiration for you to do whatever it is that feels best to you in your life. **You get to decide**! Let it be a model of power, right there in your own body, and/or in the bodies of those you choose to support in your work. And you can do it—because **you are enough**.

My final words to you, now that you know what they mean and are ready to go out and do your thing with them, changing the world as you go:

GO MILK YOURSELF!

Chapter 10:
Spreading the Love
(My Favorite Resources)

Remember how shame can be the feeling that we are unworthy of connection?

Connection is absolutely key to making your Journey to Enoughness happen.

You know how to **gather your team**. Also know that your team may include people who don't actually know you, but who may become some of your best teachers and supporters.

In this brief chapter, I've listed some of my favorite resources, along with a description of why I like them so much. Since you can't click on the links I've included below, you can find all of them with a quick search of the interWeb(b)s.

Things to Read

The Big Letdown: How Medicine, Big Business, and Feminism Undermine Breastfeeding
by Kimberly Seals Allers
So far, my training and experience supporting lactating parents, and being one myself, has left me with a lot of questions. Why is it that breastfeeding feels like such a struggle for so many? What challenges within our culture contribute to this experience? *Why is it just so damn hard?* Reading *The Big Letdown* has helped me understand why things are the way they are, for so many of us, as we strive to feed our babies with our bodies. Kimberly covers a massive

range of topics in this groundbreaking text, including the histories of pediatrics, formula, and breast pumps; an exploration of the often-conflicting research available about breastfeeding; behind-the-scenes information about businesses that contribute to the undermining of breastfeeding; and a take on feminism that is both astonishing and explains a *lot*. In short, Kimberly is a truth-teller. *The Big Letdown* is a must-read for activists and curious minds alike.

Rising Strong by Brené Brown

This book was written for anyone who has hurt to heal. Sooooo that's everyone. Brené encourages readers to dig deep into the parts of your story that have challenged you, re-examine them in ways that help you heal, and move forward, writing a "brave new ending" to those stories that will support you in living a more authentic life. At the time of this writing, the release of her next book is imminent, so this will likely be the last time I can say that this is her best work. I recommend it to every human.

You are a Badass by Jen Sincero,
and its sequel, *You are a Badass at Making Money*

Think you can't? Think again. **Jen Sincero** tells it like it is: You *are* a badass, and once you know that, you can do all the things. So go read them, you badass!

Places to Go for Support (online and in-person)

TheMilkinMama

www.themilkinmama.com

If you've read any part of this book, you know who we are. TheMilkinMama exists to support and empower anyone who feeds their babies with their bodies, and those who support them. Our website is the center of our movement. We teach the Go Milk Yourself Method, a menu of options designed to help all lactating parents hand express with confidence and ease. We work virtually (FaceTime, Skype, Zoom, you name it) and in person. We have teachers across the US and hope we will soon have teachers across the world. We run an online support group offering long-term help to anyone who takes a workshop or private session. Online Go Milk Yourself workshops run once or twice a month, more according to demand. Custom workshops are available for groups of parents, birth and lactation professionals, and other interested groups. Private sessions are available at any time, and we can find you a teacher with short notice. If you're anywhere from "curious" to "in a serious bind and need to hand express *now*," we have kind, competent humans who can help you, and we always customize our teaching for you. Videos, information about teacher trainings, resources, news articles about us, T-shirts, and more all live on our website. You can also follow us on social media @themilkinmama, or email us anytime at info@themilkinmama.com. We are here for you, always! #gomilkyourself

KellyMom
www.kellymom.com
Run by IBCLC Kelly Bonyata, Kellymom is a comprehensive resource for breast/chestfeeding parents and those who support them. Search any topic you can think of, from "fussy newborns" to "pumping at work," and you'll find exactly what you're looking for, plus resources for further reading. For answers to questions, mine and others, at all times of day, this is my go-to.

La Leche League International
www.llli.org
For free support all over the world, on the phone or in-person, individually or in a group, contact your local La

Leche League. They offer support, education, and resources to help you establish, maintain, and/or wind down breastfeeding. And they've been around *forever*!

Find a Lactation Consultant Directory
http://www.ilca.org/why-ibclc/falc
This in my favorite link on the International Lactation Consultants Association's website. Search by name, zip code, or the type of help you're seeking (a home visit, in a hospital or doctor's office, at a WIC office, volunteer help), and you'll be connected to IBCLCs near you. An awesome lactation professional can change your whole life. **You are never alone**; you deserve to receive all the support you need as you do these many impossible things.

LactMed
https://toxnet.nlm.nih.gov/newtoxnet/lactmed.htm
Want to know if a medication is safe to take while breastfeeding? Search here, and you'll find the latest research to aid you in making your decision.

A Local Breastfeeding Store or Resource Center
In NYC, we have The Upper Breast Side, Yummy Mummy, and Wild Was Mama; greater Los Angeles has The Pump Station and (my favorite!) Bini Birth. Some, such as Manhattan Birth and Baby Caravan in NYC, don't have a physical location you can just drop in to, but provide support in their beautiful spaces, or yours, at scheduled times. Many similar spaces exist across the world (and more should!). In these hubs of learning where you can take a birth or breastfeeding or baby care class, see a private lactation consultant, find the camaraderie you're craving, and get help with all the things that prove challenging, before, during, and after baby. Sit and relax for a bit—put your feet up, feed your baby. In these spaces, you can find the relief and restoration that you deserve, for a moment or the long-term. If you have one of

these magical places near you, connect, drop by, sign up. People there will help you.

People to Support You

Here are some people on my team who've really helped me get here. I'm sharing them with you so that, as you **gather your team**, you'll consider these awesome options.

Andrea Syms-Brown
www.babyinthefamily.com
As I've said a number of times in this book, Andrea is my favorite lactation consultant—the very best one I know. I'm so fortunate to have her as my mentor. If you are a lactating parent in the NYC area, or someone who lives far away and can't find an ALP you love for your team, reach out to her. She offers private sessions, in-person and virtual; incredible instruction for anyone preparing for, moving through, and winding down from breastfeeding, including continuous care (which means you have her until you and baby wean!); classes and unique support groups (called "limes") that mirror her very *real* personality, and a series of newborn care videos that are the best I've ever seen. Andrea is someone who will hear you and see you, anytime, all the time.

Tyla Fowler
www.tylafowler.com
Tyla is a light in my life, and the lives of many others. Another truth-teller, she is a human of many trades who can offering editorial services (she's the editor of this book!); coaching for your business, your life, your self; and support moving through all the challenges and desires that are uniquely yours. Working with her on this text has helped me become a stronger writer, a more confident human, and just more myself. If you're seeking support in your written work

and/or the work within you, consider her for your team. She will bring light in the places where you may feel darkness or murkiness. She'll speak the truth, and give you all of herself as you uncover and speak yours. And she'll make you laugh all the while!

Celia Behar

www.celiabehar.com
www.thelilmamas.com

Celia is a blogger and life coach, and without her coaching, I wouldn't be living this life. With a background in counseling, Celia knows how to listen, speak the truth about what she hears, and support you in living your truth. Many of her clients are now completely kicking ass at life, speaking their dreams aloud and then going after them, because of her ability to discern what you're *really* dreaming, figure out what's stopping you, and help you make and fulfill a plan to get there. Celia offers coaching sessions on the phone or in person (in California's San Fernando Valley). You can purchase them individually or in packages, as an individual or as a couple. Celia is also an expert in postpartum depression and advocate for supporting parents during that most vulnerabrave of times.

Stephanie Dawn

www.stephaniedawn.com

Stephanie is a sacred business coach who has supported me for over a year now. She is a beautiful human who radiates love—just being in her presence is a joy. For much longer than I've known her, she's supported other badass humans in taking their dreams and making them a reality. If you are ready to take your life's purpose and birth something new, perhaps something big in your life—and/or if you're already doing this and seek support reaching new levels, Stephanie can help. She offers options for one-time support and for long-term coaching, virtually or in-person, all over the world.

Samantha Moody
www.samanthaishere.com
Samantha Moody is a breathwork facilitator, doula, and birth activist. In her breathwork practice, Samantha guides individuals, couples, and groups into deep connection with stuck emotions and past traumas that can sabotage one's self-love and authenticity. Breathwork gives her clients full power over their healing process. The spontaneous healing that happens during a private or group session can result in a custom solution for their current challenge or circumstance. Samantha specializes in issues related to the childbearing year, including obstetric and chest/breastfeeding trauma. On her website and social media, be sure to check out Manageable Mindfulness, a series of audio tracks and videos focused on strategies for staying centered while adjusting to parenthood.

January Harshe
www.januaryharshe.com
You may already be familiar with January's work—she's the mom/mastermind of Birth Without Fear, Take Back Postpartum, and Find Your Village. A mom of six whose pregnancy, birth, and postpartum experiences run the gamut from traumatic to empowering, January speaks her truth in a way that connects to hundreds of thousands across the word. I tell all my clients to check out her Birth Without Fear blog and social media pages as they prepare for childbirth—I did the same as I moved through two weeks of prodromal labor with my first baby, and let me tell you, they helped me feel certain that I am indeed never alone. Check her out on social media for a daily dose of sarcasm, humor, inspiration, and general badassery.

FRANCIE WEBB

Products to Support You

I have mixed feelings about products designed to support breastfeeding woman, and the promotion of them. Many, like breastfeeding pillows, are marketed as must-haves, yet they contribute to the idea that we *can't* feed our babies with just our bodies; we need outside gadgets to make this biological process happen, to do it Right. There are also some really helpful products, like great pumps (including silicone hand pumps) and breastmilk storage bags, that I've seen make many lives easier. If you want my opinion (and I mean, you *are* reading my book), I can't think of many tangible objects you'll need to have a positive breastfeeding experience. Knowledge and support are the key. That said, there are a couple companies I really love whose missions are in line with our movement, and whose products I think are just awesome. As always, **you get to decide** what works for you!

Breastbowl

www.breastbowl.com

Breastbowl's founder, Mel, is a biomechanical engineer and mother of two in Canada who discovered that hand expression worked far better for her than an electric pump. We found each other when a friend connected us on social media, and it's been a match made in boob heaven! I mean, come on—her hashtag is #expressyourself. When Mel couldn't find a vessel that met her standards for expressing milk into, she used her skills and experience to design the original Breastbowl, and then took a glass-blowing class to learn how to make it with her own two hands. Breastbowls feature: a shape that's ergonomically pleasing to the lactating person (read: easy to hold); zero measurement lines to counter our collective scarcity issues; a spout to pour the milk in to a freezer bag or bottle; a flat spot on the bottom so it can rest on the nearest surface, and handblown glass for beauty and durability. Most recently, she launched a line of silicone Breastbowls, which are lightweight, easier to pack and travel with, and more affordable than the original version. Like a silicone hand pump, they also suction to your breast or chest so that you can catch milk on one side while nursing or pumping the other side. You can find out more at breastbowl.com.

The Dairy Fairy

shop.thedairyfairy.com
Emily, the founder of The Dairy Fairy, is a mom and ingenious entrepreneur—she's designed beautiful and functional bras that you can wear all day long, while pumping or not! You won't even notice that they have a space to secure your pump's breastshields—it's hidden behind a layer of soft fabric and lace. The Dairy Fairy products are comfortable *and* make you feel pretty fab. Emily is also quite an innovator, always looking for new ways to make lactating parents' lives easier with her products. Check out The Dairy Fairy bras and coordinating lingerie to find something that's a great match for you.

Give and Receive Milk

Humans have been sharing milk since the beginning of time. If you are a lactating parent in need of milk or with milk to share, you have options, and I encourage you to use them.

Milk Banks

At a milk bank, human milk is tested with rigorous procedures and shared with families in need. You can do a quick internet search to find one near you.

Milk Sharing

Informal milk sharing allows parents to give and receive milk when and where they need it. The sites below help connect parents who are donating and parents who are in need, mostly via local Facebook groups. If someone is in need of milk, I'm always happy to give it. If someone has milk to spare, I'm always happy to find someone who needs it, including myself. Any way you slice it, milk sharing is a gift you will never forget, and one that's so easy to give.

Eats on Feets
www.eatsonfeets.com

Human Milk for Human Babies
www.hm4hb.net

Apps
Is there an app for that? When it comes to meditation, there definitely are, and I want to share them with you!

Insight Timer
This is my favorite app for meditation. You can use a timer to track your hot dates with mindfulness, long or short (even 2 minutes every day makes a big difference!), and see your progress over time. You can also search among thousands of recorded guided meditation practices to find precisely the support you need at any given time. They have tracks dedicated to connecting with your baby while pregnant, support falling asleep, working through fear and anxiety, deep relaxation (including yoga nidra), getting kids started with meditation, and more. My favorite feature is the fact that Insight Timer shows you how many people are meditating with you using the app at the same time—it's *always* in the thousands. This helps remind us that we are never alone. If you're looking for a quick respite, a way to deepen your practice, or anything in between, Insight Timer is a great way to go. Zero experience required.

Headspace

Headspace is another great meditation app that I found helpful for getting back into my practice after I'd dropped off for a few months. It's super simple, user-friendly, and has clever animated videos designed to teach the Why behind meditation, in addition to the How. It's nice to have Headspace.

Things to Help You Heal!

If you haven't already, go read Healing into Enoughness in Chapter 6 on healing—why it's important, how it can change your life. Below are my favorite resources to support you in the process of healing.

Talk Therapy

Talk to someone whose job it is to help you heal. There are many resources on the internet to help you find a therapist who's a great match for you. Because there are so many websites that list therapists available in your area, including your own insurance company's website, I've chosen not to name any particular one here. Just know that with one quick internet search, you could be on your way to finding the support that you need to heal.

Somatic Therapies

www.emdr.com
www.traumahealing.org
www.bodymindinflow.com

Specific therapies are designed to help you get into your body, where your trauma and other life challenges live. EMDR (eye movement desensitization and reprocessing) is one I've tried recently, and it was hugely effective in helping me access and process old trauma. Somatic Experiencing® (SE) therapy helps release traumatic shock and, like EMDR, can provide support transforming trauma from the earliest stages of life through adulthood. You can search either of the first two websites above to find practitioners in your area. If you are in NYC or nearby, I highly recommend Ines Guariguata of Body Mind in Flow as a practitioner; her work integrates both of these modalities as well as others.

Bodywork

Getting in your body can help you in your Journey to Enoughness. Massage, physical therapy, cranial sacral therapy, acupuncture, myofascial release, chiropractic work, and any other experiences that feel good to you, help you. **You get to decide** which are a great match for you. A few of my favorite places and people are below; a quick search of the internet can help you find others near you.

Earth & Sky Healing Arts

www.earthsky.dreamhosters.com
Owner Katinka Locascio is a cranial sacral therapist, massage therapist, fertility awareness instructor, osteopath-to-be, and many other things, and she knows how to gather a team. Their location in Long Island City, NYC is a hub for healing no matter where you are in life.

Integrate NYC and Integrate Health and Wellness

www.integrate-nyc.com (NYC)
integrate.herbs@gmail.com *(Beacon)*
In these two practices, located in Manhattan and Beacon, NY, founders Sean Orlando, Colin O'Banion, Emily Morrison, and their colleagues provide truly integrative bodywork, including physical therapy, cranial sacral therapy, tui na, cupping, herb therapy, and more. My recent work with them has helped me heal injuries that have affected my whole life, whether I realized them or not. My favorite part of a session is when they work with the ancient practice of bone-setting. Some treatments may be covered by your insurance.

Yoga

I love yoga. Here are some of my favorite yoga places and people.

Yoga Anytime

www.yogaanytime.com

My favorite online yoga classes are on YogaAnytime, a website and an app. They are organized into episodes and seasons. Kira Sloane, Dana Flynn, Erich Schiffmann, Scott Blossom, and Alana Mitnick are a few of my favorites. You can search by duration, purpose, part of your body, style, teacher, and more. It's a fun place with options for anyone, anytime!

Harlem Yoga Studio

www.harlemyogastudio.com

If you live in or near Harlem, or you visit NYC at any point, this is where I'll send you for yoga. The space is simply peaceful, the instructors are kind and knowledgeable, the workshops and programs are designed to inspire and empower you in creating change outside and within. And they are family-friendly—my kids love their classes!

Integral Yoga

www.integralyoga.org

Classes, retreats, workshops, centers around the world, yoga for kids, grocery stores, bookstores, ashrams—Integral Yoga has it all. Following their mission of Truth is One, Paths are Many, they are loving and inclusive to beginners and seasoned practitioners of yoga. I've practiced at their institute here in NYC and visited their ashram in Virginia, and I've felt more loved and become more loving each time I go.

FRANCIE WEBB

Laughing Lotus Yoga
www.laughinglotus.com
For a wild and crazy yoga experience that's both healing and fun, this is your place. Studios in Manhattan, Brooklyn, San Francisco, and the new, donation-based Church of Yoga in New Orleans are filled with bright graffiti, great instruction, and laughter. Taking a class with founder Dana Flynn is a yoga experience like no other. So much joy!

The People Who Got Me Here (aka Acknowledgements)

WHERE DO I BEGIN?

How about with the people who, if you will, began ME right here on this Earth.

My parents, Patty and Chris Webb. When I describe you to others, new friends or strangers, I always call you "the most generous people I know." You just *give* so much to others—your time, your energy, your whole selves. What an incredible model you've provided for me about how to live in this world—with love, the most active kind of love, as givers and helpers. Thank you for believing in me well before and far more often than I have. I am because you are my parents. I love you!

To my five siblings: I once told a friend that you're the best things that's ever happened in my life. While a few others have rivaled you for that title, it's still true—by being all your very different selves, you created a space in which it was not only okay, but basically *normal* for me to be my very different self. Thank you for being mine.

To the rest of my (large, extended) family: I love you and I thank you for always loving me right back!

To my most wonderful friends, too numerous to name here—thank you for loving me as family, for all these years. I'm totally wowed that you're on my team. Please stay!

To the yoga teachers who've gotten me here: Carolyn Wilson, Natalie Levin, Bernadette Latin, Madhaven, Mataji, Kira

FRANCIE WEBB

Sloane, Alana Mitnick, Dana Flynn, Scott Blossom, Chandra Levy, Laura Tyree, Erich Schiffmann, Jason Crandell, Jess Blake, and Erica Barth: You've changed every inch of my being, and/or helped me see and love every inch of my being. Thank you for helping me learn to *live*.

To my MilkinMamas: You believed in me, invested in me, joined this movement at its very beginning. You have helped *make* Go Milk Yourself a movement. For the time you've spent in training, the workshops, the private sessions, the support for clients present and past, the ways you've pushed my thinking, the willingness to care for people you've never even met at a moment's notice, the support you've given *me* as I find my way—I am grateful. Thank you for being here. I'm so glad that you are.

To Gina Goodman and Stephanie Minnich, whose graphic design work has been integral to my exploration of self and our work this year, thank you for taking my vision and making it visual—making it ours. Specific thanks to Gina for designing a particularly badass cover that I thought was a crazy idea at first, and to Stephanie for her feedback in making it happen. It softens my heart and gives me so much peace to have you on my team. Thank you.

Lisa, my Boobsistant, your loving presence reminds me that **I am never alone**. Thank you for doing this with me.

Thank you Allison Emmett for your help with The Big Disclaimer—for being exactly what I needed at exactly the right time!

Thank you Sharon McCay for dropping everything to help me labor with this baby. You're a pretty fab book doula, I'd say!

Thank you Lindsey Rei for your final editing eye. You helped me breathe easier at a time when I thought this project may never end!

Thank you to my dear friend Emily Kelly for believing in me in Ojai, and for taking that badass milk picture, to boot!

To Laura Vladimirova of NYC Doula Love: I hired you to take photographs for the interior of this book because I knew you would get the job done. What I didn't know is that you would give me a whole new perspective on hand expression: as a thing of true beauty in addition to a hugely important skill. Thank you for your practiced eye, for your creative solutions to challenges, for being so very easy to work with, and for your never-ending support.

To the parents who bared your breasts and your souls for the photographs you see in this book: thank you for your bravery and your love—for helping to normalize this very normal thing. I'm grateful for you!

Thank you to Adam and your team at The Headshot Truck for our cover photo.

Thank you, Hassan Abdus-Salaam of Forthelovers and Shoot with Haz, for my biography headshot.

Thank you to the incomparable Daba Fall for essentially co-parenting with me during the writing of this book. I love you forever. We are family!

To Maggie Webb Meyer, my favorite sister: Thank you for writing me the perfect biography for this book. I hope you like the edits. I love you!

FRANCIE WEBB

To my incredible birth team: Karla, Kristen, Chloe, Michelle, Marisa, Rose, Krista, and Mom: Thank you for helping me, as Rose put it, train for that particular marathon, when I didn't know I was meant to cross the finish line on my own. Your support leading up to our birth cleared me of all fear, and surrounded me with the love I needed and deserved. I will never forget your role in that astonishing experience!

To my wonderful colleagues at M.S. 324, GCP, KIPP:STAR, and KIPP NYC: Thank you for always believing in me, and *still* being here for me, even as the years pass and our priorities and pursuits shift. I've been blessed with the best colleagues in the world since I began teaching, and so much of how I now lead is because of what I've learned from you. I'm grateful to have you on my team.

Celia Behar, my life coach who saw what I wasn't ready to (not even close!)—thank you. You breathed life into ideas even as I held my own breath, wishing something could change but just not knowing how or when. Your time and words and straight-up "You shoulds" have, ya know, changed my life. That's great life coaching. I will forever be grateful for the work you've put into me to help me find this perfect path.

To Stephanie Dawn—Wow. Thank you for being by my side throughout this incredible birth, which has felt quite long at times. You have been a great teacher and a true blessing to me on this journey. I've felt your love every day as I've blossomed. I am so grateful.

To Nadine, and your beautiful family: Thank you. I love you all so much!

Andrea Syms-Brown, my favorite lactation consultant in the whole world: A brilliant, perceptive soul sent me to you. She pulled me aside and said, "Don't take this hospital's breastfeeding class. Go to Andrea's." So I did, and I knew it was the start of something big. Seeing your face and hearing your voice has been a source of relief, humor, and love for the past half-decade. I had no idea how much meeting you would change my life. This book is here because I said to you, "Andrea, I really want to teach people to hand express." And you said, "Then that's what you shall do." You took time out of your schedule to come to my apartment, sit at my table with me while I nursed the same soul who was growing in my body when we met, and told me that I could do it—and even more powerful, that I *would*. Your ability to state my pipe dream as fact completely altered the course of my life, and I'm now so honored to be learning from you, from the *best*. Thank you for being in my life. Thank you for being my teacher. I can't wait to see what's next for us!

Tyla Fowler. WOW. Our baby is now earthside—go us! I call you my editor because that's the simplest way to describe our work together, to others. You are that and so many *more* things to me. I am a better writer because of you; a more authentic human because of you; more aware of my self because of you; dreaming of and counting on a more badass future because of you. In this great work, you have been my partner, and a truly great one. I love you and I'm proud of us and I am **certain** that the More we find in the future, together and individually, will change this here world. I'm so glad to have you on my Journey.

My darling Leo: Hi Baby! Where do I begin? I am so beyond grateful for you. Early in our relationship, I thought, "Wow, he lets me be me!" Now I understand that I don't need your or anyone's permission to be me. That said, your love sets me free—free to be the greatest and biggest and best and most loving me I've ever been, and getting better over time. I didn't know I deserved to be loved like this. In your love for me and our family, you never stop; you never falter. This book exists because you have so much faith in me, that you help me have faith in my *self*. Thank you for making exquisite humans with me; thank you for being my life partner; thank you for being all that you are so effortlessly, *including* a kickass dad and husband. I love you.

To my biggest girl and my littlest girlfriend: I've known many teachers in my life, and been a teacher for many. I've also shouted out a number of my favorite teachers here on these pages. When you're old enough to read this, I want you to know, now and forever, that you are the greatest of my teachers. When I stop and stare at you, it's because I can't believe you exist—that God has gifted me you. My wish is for you always to know that **you are enough**; that **you are never alone**. Believe me when I say: I'm your biggest fan. I love you so to the much.

The Big Disclaimer

I am not a medical provider. I'm also not yet, at the time of writing this book, an International Board Certified Lactation Consultant (IBCLC), though I'm working on that.

I'm a self-taught parent, an entrepreneur, a lover of learning, and a human, who's constantly seeking the balance between embodying humility and recognizing (and nurturing) my own greatness. (Some of my greatest teachers, many of whom are listed in the Acknowledgements section, might call this greatness "authenticity.")

I'm the grown-up version of the little girl who said, over and over again, "I just want to help people."

All that said, nothing I have written here should be taken as medical advice. It is up to you to **gather your team** of medical providers, wellness professionals, and other support persons, and it is also up to you to determine whose advice to follow. **You get to decide** what's right for you and your body, using the information you gather.

This book has not been approved by the FDA, CDC, AAP, WHO, ILCA, or any other official organization. My work outlined in this book has also not been funded, sponsored, or otherwise officially endorsed by any other organization. This text has been read by a number of people, including an experienced IBCLC, for accuracy and engagement.

This book contains information based on what I've learned as a teacher of hand expression, as a parent, and as a human.

FRANCIE WEBB

While this book may be providing advice on certain topics, no one knows or can understand your body better than you. If you think you should seek medical advice, please do so. **You get to decide**, and we fully support your decision. As we are not medical providers, we also encourage you to discuss anything you learn in this book with your medical provider so you can make an informed decision on the best course of action and/or treatment for yourself.

Do not rely on the information provided in this book as an alternative to medical advice from your doctor or other professional healthcare provider.

Do not delay seeking medical advice, disregard medical advice, or discontinue medical treatment solely because of information in this book. Only you and your healthcare provider(s), and other members of your team, can decide the right path for you. Again, **you get to decide.**

The information in this book is provided "as is" without any guarantees.

Reference to any products, services, or other information by trade name, trademark, supplier or otherwise does not constitute or imply its official endorsement, sponsorship, or recommendation by me. Usage is for my convenience only, in my effort to provide you with resources that have been helpful to me and those I've supported.

We exclude all representations, warranties, and conditions, and nothing contained in this Big Disclaimer will limit any of our or your liabilities in any way that is not permitted under applicable law, or exclude any of our or your liabilities that may not be excluded under applicable law.